Una Marson

THE CARIBBEAN BIOGRAPHY SERIES

The Caribbean Biography Series from the University of the West Indies Press celebrates and memorializes the architects of Caribbean culture. The series aims to introduce general readers to those individuals who have made sterling contributions to the region in their chosen field – literature, the arts, politics, sports – and are the shapers and bearers of Caribbean identity.

Other Titles in This Series

Earl Lovelace, by Funso Aiyejina
Derek Walcott, by Edward Baugh
Marcus Garvey, by Rupert Lewis
Beryl McBurnie, by Judy Raymond

UNA MARSON

Lisa Tomlinson

The University of the West Indies Press
Jamaica • Barbados • Trinidad and Tobago

The University of the West Indies Press
7A Gibraltar Hall Road, Mona
Kingston 7, Jamaica
www.uwipress.com

A catalogue record of this book is
available from the National Library of Jamaica.

ISBN: 978-976-640-696-7 (cloth)
978-976-640-697-4 (paper)
978-976-640-698-1 (Kindle)
978-976-640-699-8 (ePub)

Cover photograph of Una Marson courtesy of the
National Library of Jamaica.

Jacket and book design by Robert Harris
Set in Whitman 11.5/15

Printed in the United States of America

CONTENTS

INTRODUCTION

B orn in 1905 in rural Jamaica, Una Marson takes up poet and novelist Claude McKay's literary torch to give value to African Jamaican aesthetics and to serve as a spokesperson for the labouring class of African Jamaicans. Marson's work embodied anti-colonialism, anti-racism, feminism, class politics and pan-Africanism. Indeed, her efforts in championing Jamaican literature, as well as her avid support for Caribbean writers in Britain and the region, made her a key proponent of the development of a national and West Indian literary canon.

Marson's writings have influenced a number of Caribbean creative writers who, like herself, have used literature as an anchor to advocate cultural and political transformation in their native and host countries. Jamaican poet and academic Afua Cooper, for instance, has pointed to Marson's work as a major influence in shaping her literary and advocacy work in her adopted home of Canada. Marson's commitment to women's liberation, racial justice, class levelling, and desire to depart from British poetic models shaped a generation of writers who promoted cultural and political sovereignty. Marson belongs to a long line of black internationalists, intellectuals and activists, such as C.L.R. James, whose works have been significant in the struggles for cultural assertion and self-determination of people of African descent as well as those in Africa.

Marson's travels opened up opportunities and introduced her to many black political and cultural figures, such as Emperor Haile Selassie and Paul Robeson. The network she formed in Europe and her own personal experience with racial prejudice would help to inform her work. Marson championed African Jamaican folk materials and symbols in her work to highlight the day-to-day realities of the dispossessed majority in her homeland and in the wider African diaspora. Her literary contacts with African American writers also nourished her creativity, especially in the development of a new and distinct literary style that broke with conventional English literature.

Marson's valorization of her African Jamaican heritage and her Caribbeanization of jazz in her creative work added to her growth as a poet and playwright. She challenged and refashioned the literary convention at a time when the British cultural influence was dominant in shaping anglophone Caribbean identities.

As one of the first leading black feminists, Marson used her position to speak out against sexism and to intersect issues of race and class to articulate the struggles of women of the African diaspora. Her ideas around gender and race aimed to foster understanding and represent the diversity that made up key components of the heterogeneous nature of people of African descent. These differences are reflected in many poems in which she portrays the lives of African diaspora women through various lenses. The lonely and exoticized African Caribbean colonial migrant is depicted in her poem "Little Brown Girl", and the labour exploitation of black working-class Jamaican women is expressed in "The Stone Breakers".

Coupled with her contribution and commitment to Caribbean and British literature and culture, Marson was a central player in the transnational and intercultural conversation that Paul Gilroy has identified as "The Black Atlantic". Marson moved between Jamaica and England during the formative years of her development as a poet. Her collection of poems *The Moth and the Star* (1937) conveys the diasporic sensibilities that spoke of the tension between the West Indies and the "mother country" and underscores the collective formation of a distinctive black diaspora literary voice. Her speaker, Quashie, for instance, in the poem "Quashie Comes to London", comically reflects on his alienation in London as a Caribbean immigrant trying to culturally negotiate the terrain of his outsider status. The complex relationship between the speaker and the empire offered a fresh template for engaging in dialogue around African identities through the perspective of the Black Atlantic. The experience of in-betweenness by the homesick immigrant would also become a common thread in Caribbean diasporic fiction.

Una Marson's work spans four published collections of poetry and three plays between 1930 and 1945, and, following her involvement in the Voice series at the British Broadcasting Corporation (BBC), she established her own radio show, *Caribbean Voices*. Ironically, Marson's presence in Caribbean literature is often overlooked despite her tremendous achievment in internationalizing a Caribbean literary canon through this show. Her cultural advocacy around black nationalism is also overshadowed by African Caribbean and African American male writers such as Aimé Césaire, Claude McKay and Langston Hughes.

As with her celebrated male counterparts, pan-Africanism became a leading marker in Marson's political activism. Her pan-Africanist vision focused on educational reform on her island, a reform that aimed to see Jamaican children being taught about their African past rather than the traditional Eurocentric curriculum. Marson's creative work also reflected her pan-African political vision. Poems such as "Black Is Fancy" and "Kinky Hair Blues", in her ground-breaking collection of poetry *The Moth and the Star*, gave special attention to countering European beauty aesthetics as the standard and encouraging African racial pride for black women.

While Marson has remained on the margins of the Caribbean literary canon, Lloyd W. Brown has applauded her as the "first female poet of significance to emerge in West Indies literature".[1] Also, the emergence of black feminist literary criticism in the 1980s brought Marson's work to the fore for a new generation. More recently, Marson's plays *Pocomania* and *London Calling* have been published by Blouse and Skirt Books.

Like Claude McKay, Marson's literary and political work

was inspired by her birthplace, Jamaica, and later extended to a broader community of diasporic Africans whose desire was to claim a distinct national voice and identity. In contrast to McKay, Marson stayed in Jamaica to bear witness to the actualization of a "cultural renaissance" that would finally acknowledge and value African Jamaican culture. The 1950s and 1960s ushered in a new artistic and literary dawn for anglophone Caribbean people, as evident in the number of artists, musicians and creative writers working in and outside of the Caribbean. Writers such as Jamaican Andrew Salkey, Barbadian George Lamming and Trinidadian Samuel Selvon began to make their mark internationally as prominent Caribbean writers and cultural activists. By this time, "Una Marson had completed her life's journey of writing and social activism, and she could sit firmly at the same table with notable Black male internationalists. Working within the agenda of Black internationalist politics, Marson's lifelong work was devoted to Black self-determination, nationalism in her country, and attempts to broaden the ties between diverse African populations around the world."[2] Marson's work was instructive and ahead of its time. She boldly challenged racial inequality, affirmed standards of black beauty and black identity, and explored the complexities of gender, religious discrimination and class/economic exploitation. She did not frame her work around a single cause but, instead, she was mindful of the multiple intersections of oppression. In the end, through her advocacy and pioneering work, Marson achieved a voice for the oppressed.

ONE

Una Maud Victoria Marson was born on 6 February 1905, in Sharon village in the parish of Saint Elizabeth, Jamaica. Marson was the youngest of six children of Reverend Solomon Isaac and Ada Marson. At birth, like many Caribbean children, Marson was given a pet name by people within the community. The people of her small town gave her the pet name "Parson Baby", and even though her father registered her on 24 March as Una Maud Victoria Marson, both names stayed with her throughout her life. When Marson returned to her rural community after many years of living overseas, an elderly woman from her father's former church rushed to shower her with hugs, bawling out, "Parson Baby".[3]

Marson spent her formative years at Sharon Mission House, where she was born. The home was the property of the local Baptist church where her father worked as a minister. It was torn down in the mid-1960s, leaving little, if any, memory behind of Marson's early childhood years. What we do know about her in those years is that she was always looked after by female caregivers. Her mother, the primary female figure in her life, was a seamstress who worked at home and took care of her family. Marson, however, says little about the affection she received from her mother and the two were likely emotionally distant. Marson, in her letter titled "Cousin Angie" (*Daily Gleaner*, 9 July 1964, 3), states that there was more parental discipline in the family home at Sharon than maternal love. She recalled that "we had to learn to sit nicely, to close the door quietly, to refrain from shouting in the house and quarrelling with one another as children are sometimes apt to do". Jenny DaCosta, a long-time family friend, shares some insight on the relationship between Marson and her mother: "They were opposites in their physical appearance and in their views on life." Una Marson was "quite different. She was very down to earth and wasn't a bit like them." Edith Marson, the elder sister, "took after Marson's mother in manner and appearance: both were tall and of light complexion". Una Marson was no doubt the odd one out because "her modernity would be traceable in her sexual curiosity, her idiosyncratic dress, her inglorious needlecraft and her years in 'exile' " (*Life*, 8). Despite this contrast and indifference to her mother, Marson dedicated a touching poem to her after her death. "My Mother" was first published in the *Cosmopolitan* magazine, owned by Marson. In the dedication, she laments,

> Oh! my Mother, my Mother, I hear the bells ring,
> And the glad Christmas carols the dear children sing;
> But my thoughts turn to you and the teardrops will start,
> For I miss your sweet presence to comfort my heart.

CHAPTER ONE

Oh! my Mother, my Mother can you hear me call?
Can you see the heartache, the tears as they fall?
I know that Christ sees them, but Mother of mine,
It is so hard without you, sweet Mother Divine.

While there was a void of maternal love between Marson and her mother, Una found consolation in her immense love for her cousin Angie Solomon, for whom she expressed deep admiration. Cousin Angie was Una's favourite visitor to the Marsons' home. Angie was single and independent; she owned a fabric store and would always bring material for dresses on her visit to the Marsons. Marson recalls that "this was chosen with great care as to patterns and colour. And of course, there was a tie for Cousin Sol" (*Daily Gleaner*, 9 July 1964, 3). Angie's visits were once or twice a year and she often stayed a few weeks at a time. Her visits were filled with love and vibrancy. Marson enjoyed the news, gossip and lively conversations that lightened the house during her visits. Angie would spend late nights with Marson's parents recounting stories about relatives and church members. With the younger cousins, including Marson, Angie exchanged bedtime and ghost stories "and we were not frightened one bit", Marson notes in the *Gleaner* article. Throughout the years, Marson maintained contact with Angie and the two remained close, although they rarely got to see and spend time with each other. Angie died after a short illness in May 1964.

Marson also spent time with her maternal grandmother growing up, but it was her cousin Angie who had the greatest impact on her. In fact, Marson's admiration for Angie's free-spirited nature may have served as a blueprint for how

Marson later chose to live her own unconventional life. Marson's lifestyle did not conform to the societal expectations of a woman's role. In a note, Marson highlights her cousin Angie as "one of the rare and significant daughters of the land' and 'of a type not uncommon in Jamaica'" (*Life*, 7). All this was in contrast to Marson's mother, Ada, who embodied the spirit of femininity, "but for Una, the Parson's Baby, this adult feminine world often seemed alien and inaccessible. As an adult she vacillated between shyness and anger at pretty, cultured femininity, and prised herself out of its narrowness. But she was born female and was never totally free of feminine conventions although her lifestyle was more like a man's. She was her father's daughter-son" (*Life*, 9).

Marson's unconventional "feminine" behaviour could have been nurtured through a much closer bond that she had with her father. Unlike her sisters Edith and Ethel, who resembled their mother, Marson shared similar physical characteristics with her father and she was interested in many of the same things as he, things that would be traditionally of interest to men. This similarity with her father may have allowed Marson "to live an independent life as sons of robust fathers are said to live".

Even though Marson was different from her mother and sisters, they all shared a love for the arts and the gift and talent for creative writing: "All the Marson women and girls were talented in the literary and performing arts. Ada, their mother, was an accomplished organist and frequently played for church services, a skill particularly admired in a parson's wife and encouraged in parson's daughters. Ethel, whose greatest hobby was always music, also learnt to play well" (*Life*, 9–10).

The Marson children began to read at an early age and enjoyed reading. In addition, Marson and her sisters would playfully make up verses for games they invented. Their home was filled with a wide range of classical literature and they were exposed to different genres. This immersion in literature, and her early appreciation for it, established Marson's avid interest in the art of writing. More significantly, she took advantage of her father's library and read from his collection of religious books. At an early age, Marson read works by Henry Wadsworth Longfellow, including *Hiawatha*, *Evangeline* and *Tales of a Wayside Inn*, and she read *Men of Backbone* by Reverend C.A. Wilson. Marson's early exposure to such classics and her talent in the performing arts would later prepare her for a prestigious education at Hampton School, an all-girls boarding school in rural Saint Elizabeth, Jamaica.

Marson was enrolled in Hampton School at age ten. Her father was a member of the school's board of trustees until his passing in 1915. Hampton was an elite and conservative boarding school for primarily upper-middle-class white and light-skinned girls, and it was known for its educational excellence. With extensive coaching from her sisters, Marson passed her entrance examinations successfully and benefited from a Free Foundationer scholarship that she won in 1915.

Marson's years at Hampton School helped her to develop an awareness of race and class as she observed the racial differences and prejudices directed toward dark-skinned girls. The Free Foundationers recipients were mainly black Jamaican girls, like Marson, and they were "tortured by Maud Marion [Barrows, the headmistress,] who never missed an opportunity to make them stand before the whole school for a berating for any minor misdemeanour. They were continually reminded that they were getting their education free."[4] Marson's light-skinned sisters were favoured by the school teachers and administrators. Skin colour had long been a basis for social discrimination in Jamaica. Although slavery had been abolished, the legacy of contempt for dark skin was present throughout society and negatively affected how many Jamaican people felt about themselves. Lighter-skinned Jamaicans were commonly favoured over their darker-skinned compatriots.

As she grew older, Marson had conflicting ideas about the colonial education she received while attending Hampton. Although she took on pan-African politics in her literary and social activist work, she would later write a poem titled "To Hampton", in which she seems almost nostalgic:

Ah me, the cares of Latin and French,
And of the long hours spent upon the bench,
The toils of writing prose and conning rhymes
To us no doubt, did seem large ones at times
. . . .
How oft in dreams I live those days again,
Chasing a hockey ball with might and main,
Or sit and list without a thought of fear
To dearest Mona reading great Shakespeare[5]

Marson was not considered as academically bright as her sisters, who excelled at Hampton. One of the reasons noted for Marson's poor academic performance was the death of her father in 1915. The death of Solomon Marson meant that the family lost their esteemed social status and financial security. In the article "Cousin Angie" (*Daily Gleaner*, 9 July 1964, 3), Marson writes, "this meant the breaking up of our home. Three of us had to go to Hampton, one to Westwood and one to Calabar. We were growing up fast and so we moved to Kingston where two of Mother's sisters had long since settled. For us, it was the end of an era and the beginning of another."

Indeed, as Marson describes it, this period was the beginning of another chapter when she was forced to grow up quickly and to become an independent young girl. In fifth form, Marson completed courses in commercial skills and managed to pass the Oxford and Cambridge Boards' Lower Certificate. However, she had no desire to obtain the Higher Certificate like her older sister Ethel, who received distinctions in Latin and French, and went on to become a teacher. Edith, the eldest, had taken a similar academic path, successfully completing her studies to become a teacher.

In the summer of 1922, Marson left Hampton to enter the world of work. In her passing-out interview with headmistress Maud Barrows, Marson recalls how, in the eyes of Barrows, she took the wrong career path and appeared an underachiever and foolish:

> She asked me what I planned to do. I told her that as my father was dead and I wanted to help my mother, I should probably study stenography and get a secretarial job.

She was very angry. "Only fools learn shorthand," she said. "Why can't you take up teaching as your sisters have done?"

I trembled. I just knew I couldn't teach and had no idea of any other career.[6]

Marson moved to Kingston in 1922 and joined her mother and two sisters who had been living there since the death of Solomon Marson. In the capital city, Marson was first employed as a volunteer social worker with the Young Men's Christian Association and with the Salvation Army. Soon after, Marson worked as a secretary, which was one of the few professional jobs beginning to open up to black Jamaican women. At age twenty, Marson started working as assistant editor for the political journal the *Jamaica Critic*. However, Marson felt her work at the *Critic* limited her to feminine subjects by its anti-feminist owner T. Dunbar Wint, a restriction that prevented her from fully exploring social commentaries, which would later become her trademark preoccupation. Her experience as a secretary and editor helped Marson carve out her skills as a writer and led to the establishment of an independent monthly magazine called the *Cosmopolitan*, the official publication of the Jamaica Stenographers' Association. Marson, herself a stenographer, was one of the founders and the main editor and writer for the magazine.[7]

More importantly, Marson's passion highlighted the inequalities of colonial Jamaica and prompted her to expand the topics covered by her magazine as controversial issues were not always well received at the *Jamaica Critic*. The *Cosmopolitan* gained financial backing from a local businessman, George Bowen, and it was the first of its kind in Jamaica to be started and edited by a Jamaican woman. In her editorial for the first issue, Marson proudly reminded subscribers that "this is the age of woman: What man has done women may do." The magazine became a major outlet to politicize feminist views, as well as cultural and literary topics. "Our chief aim," she wrote in the first issue, "is to develop literary and other artistic talents in our Island home. . . . Our ambition is to do all we can to encourage talented young people to express themselves freely" (*Life*, 30). Short stories, poetry and commentary about current events were included in every issue. The magazine also offered a glimpse of Marson's literary talent.

Marson's values and opinions, often radical for the 1920s, were regularly shared with the readers. In the sports column, she complained about the lack of interest women showed in sports: "they seem to be content to watch the young men excel in this connection", and she encouraged her female readers to become involved in tennis and hockey.[8] In running her own magazine, Marson had a platform for showcasing issues related to the struggle and empowerment of women. She featured profiles of female musicians, such as the pianists Sybil and Noele Foster-Davis, and she provided announcements of conferences about women. Her feminist work included advocacy for women's suffrage in Jamaica, for the broadening of opportunities in education and employment, and for the advancement of inclusive self-help groups for women.

Marson did not shy away from issues of race. She pointed out the racism and colourism that permeated colonial Jamaica; she had endured the same colourism during her years at Hampton School. In 1931, when a blonde, blue-eyed contestant won the Miss Jamaica beauty pageant, Marson, writing in her column in the *New Cosmopolitan* (as it had been rebranded in early 1931), gave her congratulations and then commented sarcastically that perhaps "some amount of expense and disappointment could be saved numbers of dusky ladies who, year after year, enter the Beauty competition if the promoters of the contest would announce in the daily press that very dark or 'black beauties' will not be considered". She concluded: "There is a growing feeling that 'Miss Jamaica' should be a type of girl who is more truly representative of the majority of Jamaicans" (*Life*, 32).

Marson's sensitivity to issues of colourism also stemmed from her own insecurity, brought on by her family, which she carried throughout her life:

> All her life Una's physical appearance was a source of conflict and pain. She was conscious of her dark skin even after she found, in adult life, that there was beauty in blackness. In Jamaica fair skin was and is associated with beauty, charm and womanliness. It is only a small step from this notion to the idea that black also equates with dullness, stupidity and likely failure. Una never felt she was quite as clever as her fairer, elder sisters. (*Life*, 8)

Marson would later include the issue of race and of black beauty in many of her poems published after the first two volumes, *Tropic Reveries* and *Heights and Depths*. Her work from the years before her first journey to Britain demonstrated an understanding of the activities of English feminists and a commitment to an international women's movement, while she lightly covered issues related to race, cultural identity and the so-called colour bar. By the late 1930s, her literary and non-fiction writings increasingly featured these themes together with, not in place of, feminist concerns.

Although Marson's feminist interests took centre stage, she also used the magazine as a platform to voice other social concerns, such as the exploitation of the black Jamaican labouring class, who received meagre wages and lived in impoverished conditions, and the poor development of local industries. Marson's articles on these topics clearly recognized the wide class disparity between rich and poor Jamaicans. In her defence of the exploited farmers and the vast wasted land space, Marson spoke to the underdevelopment of the agricultural sector when she wrote:

> Anyone who has the opportunity of travelling through even a few of the parishes of the island will have noticed the thousands of acres of land lying idle, and if it was at the time when guavas or oranges were in season, they would have seen much of these going to waste. We mention those particularly because so much could be done to make a real industry of preserves but there are many other fruit, Cheremelias, Roseapples, Jew Plums . . . and others which would also make wonderful jams and jellies. The guava jelly and the dolce and orange marmalade are, however, the best known . . . and those which have been sent to England or America . . . attracted attention and created a demand. . . .

Is there any feasible reason why this industry could not be developed and protected? (*Life*, 36)

The magazine allowed Marson to take politics and nation building seriously. She was not impressed with Jamaica's political system, which consisted of old men who lacked the political vision and drive to improve the lives of black working-class Jamaicans. Marson, however, drew attention to Marcus Garvey, whose black nationalist, economic empowerment and self-reliance and race pride projects had exploded on the Jamaican political scene. Garvey's bringing to the fore the social abuses would in no time "prompt Marson to take him seriously": "The powers of leadership are given to few. Mr M. Garvey has these gifts. . . . Mr Garvey's methods of helping [Jamaica] may not be methods that others would adopt. But the world is large enough for every man to work out his own individual ideas – and it is the spirit of love, sacrifice and devotion that must always be the dominant factor" (*Life*, 37). Marson's "own cultural awakening probably took place at this time as Garvey's activity at Edelweiss Park was at its height and she participated in poetry presentations there".[9]

Of great significance was the platform the *Cosmopolitan* provided in support of a national literary culture. She was active in the Jamaica Poetry League and used her magazine to promote Jamaican writers in all genres: poetry, short stories and novels. While the magazine was short-lived, it published the work of several new writers who later became major Jamaican literary luminaries.[10]

By 1930, sales of the *Cosmopolitan* had fallen and advertisers were reluctant to provide financial support because of economic uncertainty worldwide as a result of the Great Depression. On Marson's part, she was unable to meet some of her personal needs and she was under pressure to produce a trendier magazine that featured more "society groups". This expectation was not in line with Marson's ideological leanings, however: "We are aware, and too well aware of the fact that magazines of the standard to which we aspire are never 'best sellers' though several times during the year just closed we disposed of our entire issues" (*Life*, 38).

Marson was fortunate to keep the magazine operating with the assistance of Aimee Webster, a graduate hailing from the planter class. Webster became the co-editor and took on half of the financial burden. This was good news for Marson, who had no financial means to contribute to the operation of the magazine and was still doing other jobs on the side. In February 1931, the magazine was redesigned and published as the *New Cosmopolitan*. The facelift, however, was not enough to save the magazine and by April 1931, Marson wrote: "It is with a deep sense of regret that I make the announcement that the publication [of the *New Cosmopolitan*] is now postponed for an indefinite period. I say indefinite because I cannot foresee how long the present depression will last. . . . I very much regret having to do this but have no alternative." Both Webster and Marson were deeply saddened by the discontinuation of the magazine. In an interview years later, Webster alleged that Marson had been dishonest in handling funds earned from the magazine: "On the plantation I had lived a very sheltered life and had not discovered this rascality before, which is a characteristic of all Jamaicans of all races. Una left to collect monies from advertisers and then used it to pay her personal bills, leaving me with the magazine's bills and she migrated soon after" (*Life*, 38–39).

Before migrating to England in 1932, Marson published her first book of poetry, *Tropic Reveries* (1930) and staged her first play, *At What a Price* (1930). Marson's poems were met with mixed reviews. Her poetry relied quite heavily on the British literary aesthetic from her education at Hampton School and she was criticized for her overly passionate love poems and for her uneven use of language.

Marson's second collection of poetry, *Heights and Depth* (1931), encountered similar challenges and continued the display of her colonial education and the underlying implication of British superiority and West Indian inferiority. In addition, she worked within a framework of acceptable subjects for female poets: love and nature. Marson's poetic themes were contrary to the political conviction she expressed in the *Cosmopolitan* and her general activism. She would have to overcome restrictions and learn to trust her own voice in order to write on issues that dealt with Jamaica and the wider Caribbean. That growth would take place after Marson left Jamaica: her travels expanded her knowledge and helped her centre her activism on issues of gender, race and class.

As the publishing prospects in early-twentieth-century Jamaica (and the rest of the region) were limited, Caribbean creative writers were unable to make a decent living from their craft. As V.S. Naipaul described it, "writing in Trinidad was an amateur activity. . . . There were no magazines that paid; . . . there was only The [Trinidad] Guardian."[11] The situation in Kingston, Jamaica, was no better because "not a single bookstore existed in Kingston, Jamaica in 1930".[12] Unlike her compatriot Claude McKay, who travelled to the United States and established a successful writing career, moving to the United States was not an option for Marson. She was aware of the struggles black women faced trying to earn a living in the United States and decided, instead, to migrate to what was known at the time as the Mother Country. Although Marson's "worst nightmare was to end up working in someone else's kitchen, reigning over greasy pots and pans, storecupboards, brushes and mops", she took the bold step to leave her country of birth to move to an unknown terrain that she had only read about in books:

> And so Una had settled on England. England had captured her imagination. It was the birthplace of Keats and Shelley, the land of gracious living. Her naïve and youthful mind was enchanted. Her personal strength, her "zest to taste life all at once", a quality which a forgiving Aimee Webster was later to pinpoint, convinced Una to make the Atlantic leap. When on 9 July 1932 Una arrived in Plymouth, England, on board SS *Jamaica Settler*, her pockets lined with the slender profits from *At What a Price*, she was, so she later claimed, intending to stay for a three-month holiday. Four years later, by the summer of 1936, she was still living in London, weary and, in her own words, "heading for a nervous breakdown caused by overwork". (*Life*, 44–45)

TWO

Una Marson arrived in England in 1932, at age twenty-seven. For Marson, her experience in London was bittersweet. While her career would strengthen from here onward, she was ill-prepared for the racial prejudice that awaited her, such as the "please no coloured" signs Naipaul mentions in *The Middle Passage*.[13] Her first experience exposed her to the harsh realities of British racial prejudice and would significantly shape her outlook on England. As a colonial Jamaican, Marson unquestioningly viewed herself as a British subject, but her reception in Britain was far from one welcoming a "native daughter". She retells an incident in a poem involving a group of white children shouting the racial epithet "Nigger" at her as she strolled along the streets of London. This verse is filled with the vivid imagery of Marson's anger and the pain she endures:

> They called me "Nigger",
> Those little white urchins,
> They laughed and shouted
> As I passed along the street,

They flung it at me:
"Nigger! Nigger! Nigger!"

What made me keep my fingers
From choking the words in their throats?
(*Keys* 1, no. 1 [1933])

There was some naivety on Marson's part, as this encounter surely must have been a collective experience for other racialized emigrants from the colonies who were also taught that they were British subjects. But once they migrated, the truth of British racism suddenly became a reality. After her migration to England, Marson met "the long-imagined cultural mother who rejects her wooly headed children".[14]

Garvey would refer to Marson's disillusionment with Britain in support of his view of England:

> Our countrywoman Miss Una Marson went to England some time ago to be disillusioned. She thought she was going to a country where she would be accepted on equal terms with those who built it and made its civilization possible. Like most of our race, she thought we have nothing else to do than project ourselves into the civilization of other people and to claim all its right. When she found a contrary attitude, she rebelled and wrote some nasty things about the English.[15]

Five years later, when Marson returned to Jamaica, she shared her painful experiences of isolation in the national newspaper, the *Daily Gleaner* (28 September 1936, 5). She recounted that she had "been very hurt by some slights caused by the ignorance of people. They point at you and stare at you and it is very embarrassing. . . . In London everyone seems far off. You see groups of people and no one you know. It is very lonely."

Marson was subjected to other forms of blatant racial discrimination and disappointment in England – this time it was while looking for suitable employment. These were the barriers Marson thought she had escaped when she decided not to travel to and settle in the United States. In an unpublished article, "Problems of Coloured People in Britain", Marson protested, "the young coloured woman has to face many problems. . . . In London, most avenues of work except that of entertaining in the dance or Music halls, are closed to coloured people. . . . I myself have experienced difficulty in finding work when I urgently needed it." She continued, "I tried to register for work as a stenographer. One agent told me she didn't register Black women because they would have to work in offices with white women. Another agent tried to find me a position and he told me that though my references were excellent, firms did not want to employ a Black stenographer."[16]

Despite the hostility and dissatisfaction Marson met on her first journey to England, she ultimately became a driving force in the women's movement and the Caribbean immigrant community in London. In the metropole, she joined fellow Jamaican Harold Moody's multi-racial organization, the League of Coloured Peoples.

Not long after Marson's arrival in Britain, she began sporting the style of a contemporary, bohemian woman. According to J.P. Green, "'Black middle-class women who were born in

Britain, like Amy Barbour James, a friend of Una's who lived in Acton, 'were not expected to fully participate in political matters but to be artistic and civilised, ideal wives for professional men.'" This was contrary to Marson, who "didn't fit anywhere" (*Life*, 48). Her inability to belong was a daunting reality she had to deal with throughout her childhood and adolescent years. As an adult, Marson now had the full freedom of self-expression, freedom had been denied to her because of her religious family background and conservative colonial education. Her fashion taste came out of her fascination with Africa and African culture. Jamaican-born Sylvia Lowe recalled, "She liked to look African. She put her hair as they did . . . natural, not plaited, and combed out." Marson's style of clothing also began to morph into brighter colours as she frequently window-shopped at London's fashionable West End boutiques in search of dresses with distinctive patterns and bold accessories. Lowe pointed out that Marson's personal style was connected to her shift in political views that leaned toward pan-African politics and interest in African current affairs and stated, "She also had a good African flair and was more interested in them [Africans] than in our own affairs . . . she was a bit ahead of most people but we didn't think of that in those days" (*Life*, 48). Marson's alteration of her hairstyle was her political statement to show that she embraced African beauty standards. Her rejection of received notions of the Eurocentric myth of beauty later became central in some of her African-centred poems that spoke to the way the media diminished African beauty aesthetics or standards.

Come, I will let you go
When black beauties
Are chosen for the screen;
That you may know
Your own sweet beauty
And not the white . . .
(*Moth*, 88)

Marson's encounter with Prince Ofori Atta from Ghana also ripened her interest in Africa's history and politics. Marson "came to the realisation that Africa mattered: that its cultures, people and wisdoms equalled those of Europe and that, without the persistent attention of African people, its history would be lost, neglected and denied" (*Life*, 73).

Marson's gradual shift to black internationalism in the imperial metropole remained tied to her new-found appreciation and love for her African heritage. Her years of feeling inferior because of her dark complexion were challenged with poems that offered agency to herself and the wider African diaspora:

I am black
And so I must be
More clever than white folk,
More wise than white folk,
More discreet than white folk,
More courageous than white folk.
(*Moth*, 93)

Marson's frustration in not being able to secure a job led her to working with the League of Coloured Peoples as its unpaid assistant secretary. By this time in her life, Marson was used to working for little or nothing. What mattered to her most was the opportunity to gain any sort of employment that would allow her to pursue the things she enjoyed – writing and political activism. At the League of Coloured Peoples, she was responsible for organizing student activities, receptions, meetings, trips, and concerts, and she wrote for the *Keys*, the league's newsletter. The *Keys* provided her with a forum to write about current global affairs and racial discrimination in England and abroad, and to vent her anger and frustration about the racism she experienced. The newsletter also gave Marson the space to feature her literary work and to create a transatlantic dialogue around literature by introducing African American writers such as Zora Neale Hurston and Countee Cullen to its readers. Given the fact that England's racist environment was alienating for many West Indian and African students, the League of Coloured Peoples offered Marson security, and it served as her community.

> This is where Moody's League stepped in. At first it had been little more than headed stationary, but, by the time Una needed its comfort, a diet of social events was being planned to help such confused aliens – colonial students, visitors and dignitaries: a genteel, compensatory social calendar. During the cold winter months there were small parties at the house, cultural trips, political conferences and endless meetings. When summer came, regular tennis parties were held on the grass court at Peckham, moonlight rambles and respectable dances. (*Life*, 50)

While the League of Coloured Peoples was a social haven for Marson, she remained on the periphery, socially and ideologically. Dr Robert Wellesley Cole, a Sierra Leonean, recalled that she "gained a reputation of being 'a true loner who didn't exactly seek out company', and some League members countered by refusing to take notice of her". Cole described Marson as "extremely charming, but not one of us" (*Life*, 53).

Even though Marson did not quite "fit" into the culture of the league, she remained loyal to its members, especially to Harold Moody. Her loyalty to Moody resulted in conflicts with African American Paul Robeson in 1935 because Marson feared that he "would lead the mass of [black] students [in London] away from Moody's reformist politics . . . and toward communism" (*Life*, 94). Moody, a political moderate and ardent Christian, was opposed both by more radical pan-Africanists such as C.L.R. James and by Marxists such as Ras Makonnen (alias of the Guyanese pan-Africanist leader George Griffiths).

Marson did not neglect her feminist politics in London. She joined some women's organizations through which she formed a solid network. And she became a close friend with white feminist and novelist Winifred Holtby, who was a supporter in the struggle for racial justice. While the League of Coloured Peoples afforded Marson the platform to write about topical issues, the women's organizations heightened her career as a public speaker: "Britain's many women's organisations called Una up to make speeches. She was always happy to accept invitations and by 1936 had developed a wide range of contacts within the Women's Freedom League, the Women's Peace Crusade, the Women's International Alliance and the British Commonwealth League, of which she became an ordinary member, attending many meetings, speaking at conferences" (*Life*, 72).

One of Marson's greatest public speaking engagements was perhaps at the Twelfth Annual Congress of the International Alliance of Women for Suffrage and Equal Citizenship, held in Istanbul, Turkey, in 1935. This event was cited as the occasion where Marson delivered her most emotional speech ever. In her lecture, she passionately demanded that white feminists recognized the struggle of black people across the world as she highlighted that, "even in London one sometimes sees discrimination against black people, even those who are British subjects. Negroes are suffering under enormous difficulties in most countries in the world" (*Life*, 90). Marson's speech was well received by an audience of white women as she got "tumultuous applause" and media attention from British newspapers complimenting her on her intellect and the new challenge of race that she introduced to feminist thought. This event was also momentous, because she was the first black woman to attend the conference. In the same year, Marson's work experience at the League of Coloured Peoples facilitated her most exciting political advocacy as she landed a short-term job with the League of Nations in Geneva, where she became the first black collaborator.

Marson's work with the League of Nations proved to be a demanding period for her. This position would also represent a moment in politics that altered the course of her life in both a negative and positive way. The League of Nations offered her the opportunity to work closely with His Imperial Majesty Haile Selassie, witnessing first-hand his final pleas before the league for intervention after Ethiopia (then Abyssinia) was overrun by Italian fascist forces. After Marson's position ended with the League of Nations, the mounting crisis of Italy's territorial aggression consumed most of her attention and she developed a burning desire to assist Ethiopians in their fight against European domination. Marson was driven by her pan-African political commitments and her anti-imperialist sentiment began to grow. At that time, Ethiopia was the only African nation not colonized by Europe. Equally, its history as the oldest continuously existing African state signified the country's symbolic and substantive value to the emancipation of black people on the continent and the African diaspora. Marson knew only too well what it would mean for an African country to be defeated by a fascist Italy. She immediately approached the head of the Abyssinian delegation, Tekle Hawariat, to offer her assistance; Hawariat directed her to Dr Charles Martin, the country's ambassador to Britain. On 2 October 1935, the day before Italy's invasion of Ethiopia, Marson returned to London to take up her new post (as the English-speaking secretary to the ambassador), which focused mainly on public relations activities. No one would have ever known the meagre earnings Marson received in this position. She eagerly threw herself into her job, labouring long hours. By the end of the year, Britain supported Italy in the Hoare-Laval Pact, which was detrimental to Abyssinia. England's political appeasement of a fascist territorial attack on this African country did not stop Marson from assisting the Abyssinian cause. She was committed to preserving the African nation's independence and played a vital role in this campaign. When Haile Selassie travelled to Geneva to appeal for the defence of his country's sovereignty, she accompanied him and went on to provide secretarial support to Selassie. Down to his very last fight against the colonial power, Marson remained loyal and lauded the emperor's "indomitable will . . . to fight to the last", but confessed, "for myself, I regret to say that I am not hopeful about his fight" (*Daily Gleaner*, 28 September 1936, 5).

Marson's involvement in the Abyssinian crisis strengthened her identification with Africa and reaffirmed her commitment to black unity globally. This event also informed her outlook on the major political developments of the late 1930s. In response to news of the executions of Joseph and Benjamin Martin, the sons of Charles Martin, the Ethiopian minister, Marson penned the touching elegy "To Joe and Ben (Brutally murdered in April 1937 at Addis Ababba [*sic*] by the Italians)". The brothers had fought under the leadership of Ras Imru in a series of successful battles before ultimately being captured along with Imru:

> They sent you forth
> From "England's pleasant land",
> Home of your fond adoption,
> Of early boyhood's years –
> They sent you forth
> To the battle's front
> To fight for a country
> Yours, and yet not yours
> By unfamiliarity.
> (*Moth*, 81)

Even though the outcome of the crisis was emotionally and politically overwhelming for Marson, her effort in assisting the Abyssinian cause did not go unrecognized in her homeland. The *Daily Gleaner* (25 September 1936, 17) described Marson as "the Jamaican girl who made history for her country and race, in being the first coloured girl to be one of the collaborators at the League of Nations in Geneva". The commendation bestowed on Marson was not enough to bolster her emotional health as she fell into a severe depression and headed back to Jamaica.

In an interview on the day of her arrival in Jamaica, she told the *Daily Gleaner* (25 September 1936, 17) that "the position of Ethiopia is very heart-breaking and the tribulations of the Ethiopians have cracked me up". Marson's political naivety left her distraught and distrustful of Britain. Britain's demonstration of inter-imperialist cooperation and loyalty when it came to African self-determination would be Marson's final eye-opener. She was now forced to free herself of her colonial trappings – trappings that were in many ways responsible for much of the suffering she had experienced in England:

> Una's early belief system had taken a bashing. She had undergone an enormous transformation: now she distrusted "Europe" and looked to "Africa", and to a greater degree she looked to herself. It was not simply a question of externals. Britain's role within the League of Nations had sustained a vital emotional currency for Una, and the reality of its failure to save Abyssinia carried an inflated value for her. Although she had been intellectually prepared for life in England, nothing had prepared her emotionally and socially for the complex web of political

manoeuvrings she had witnessed, or for the harshness of racism or the feelings of isolation. Her personal age of innocence about the "Mother Country" was over. (*Life*, 104–5)

When Marson returned to Jamaica for a brief period between 1936 and 1938, Jamaica and the wider anglophone Caribbean were experiencing the assertion of the working-class against class and racial exploitation under British colonialism:

> There were strikes and rioting by sugar workers in Saint Kitts and British Guiana, charcoal burners in Saint Lucia, oilfield workers in Trinidad, dockworkers in Barbados and Jamaica. At one level these disturbances were a spontaneous outburst of the laboring class for fair wages and improved working conditions. But at a deeper level the riots represented the first concentrated attack upon colonialism, the first stirring of a people to assert their readiness for self-determination and nationhood.[17]

Political exposure from her travels abroad had sharpened Marson's intellectual ideas even more deeply. One of the first things she observed on her return home was the unchanged conditions of black working-class Jamaicans. The poverty she witnessed was exacerbated by the worldwide economic depression. She carped that "with its decorative upper crust and its impoverished masses, it was revoltingly hopeless. 'Kingston is repulsive and its people beyond redemption.' . . . and people were 'on the whole much poorer than they were when I left in '32'" (*Life*, 108). The poverty and hopelessness motivated Marson to further work toward her country's self-determination and nationhood, and she expressed this in her work.

Though discontented and disappointed by the impoverished condition of the island, Marson was energized by the nationalist movements. During her short visit to Saint Elizabeth, she decided to refocus her politics on dismantling oppressive systems of colonial legacy. Marson was reunited with her sister Etty and they ended up living together in Kingston. Marson, in short order, took on a number of leading roles in various capacities. For example, she had a column in the newly established weekly magazine *Public Opinion*, where she was the lone woman. Not surprisingly, she continued to highlight the concerns of women and, more meaningfully, she encouraged women to participate in politics. In her debut piece in *Public Opinion* ("Some Things Women Politicians Can Do", 20 February 1937), Marson asked, "Should our women enter politics?" And she answered, "A thousand times yes! . . . A start should be made at once. We must stop saying our City Council, our Legislative Council are no good – anyone can criticise. I believe our women . . . could outdo our men in politics – I throw out the challenge – who will be our first woman politician?" (*Life*, 113).

In addition to writing her feminist column, Marson became more vocal about her concerns with class politics. She used the opportunity in *Public Opinion* to challenge classism, which she felt was a greater concern in Jamaican society than the racial prejudice she had left behind almost a decade earlier. This was despite the fact that Marson herself had belonged to the League of Coloured Peoples in London, an organization that consisted largely of multi-racial and middle-class Caribbean intellectuals. Nonetheless, the class division she was greeted with in Jamaica displeased her immensely because members of this group were doing nothing to challenge the class system that exploited and dominated the labouring classes: "Officially there was no colour prejudice in Jamaica, but there was considerable class prejudice, Una had told feminists back in London in summer 1934. Home again, she was getting a taste of it. Her place, she found, was among the agitating middle classes, the equivalents of the English grammar-school set, bright, ambitious and realistic, but without the collateral or connections to revolutionise society in their favour" (*Life*, 111).

Marson found herself actively working to challenge Jamaica's colonial establishment, which painted pejorative images of everything distinctly African. She was equally disturbed in the way that many African Jamaicans accepted themselves as inferior and accepted the damaging denial of African ancestry: "Are we the young generation to remain resigned to the shame and shallowness of the artificial life into which we have been cast? Are we to remain strangers in our own land, eaters of the crumbs that fall from the table of others when we have it in our powers to sit at a table well garnished by our hands."[18]

Marson connected with other black nationalist advocates on the island, such as Amy Bailey, to address the race problem. While there might have been differences between the two women, they worked together to challenge the leadership of white upper-class women. They also developed the Jamaica Save the Children Association (Jamsave), an organization that provided economic development support to poor children and their families.

With nationalism at its peak, it was expected that a movement for pride in Jamaican arts would eventually spring up. Edna Manley, the famous sculptor and wife of Norman Manley, along with poet and scholar Philip Sherlock, were at the forefront of this movement. Marson would soon be a key spokesperson for Jamaican arts. Marson was no stranger to the museums in Europe and she knew well how England endowed its archives and treasured its heritage. Marson envisioned a break from centuries of a Eurocentric model via a cultural renaissance that would foster a national literature as its core. She championed the development of a Jamaican publishing house that would open up a market for Jamaican manuscripts. "We are passing through the birth pains of bringing forth a new Jamaica," she wrote. "In this era literature must take its place; indeed, the writing and production of books by us about ourselves and our problems is essential."[19] Her vision would eventually materialize with the creation of the Pioneer Press, a publishing house for Jamaican authors, but not for another fifteen years.

Although it took fifteen years to develop the island's own press, in her quest for a national literature in 1937, Marson's third published book of poetry, which focused mainly on Afrocentric themes, became the crucial step in her campaign to counter African inferiority on the island and to move toward a cultural renaissance in Jamaica. The country's own press would not only help to publish local writers but it would also encourage the publication of materials that depicted the cultural landscape of the people which would be inclusive of black Jamaican aesthetics. About this time, in an effort to mobilize young African Jamaican artists and writers, Marson also co-founded the Readers and Writers Club, a quasi-political literary group.

In 1937, Marson's third collection of poems, *The Moth and the Star* was published. As she embarked on establishing a cultural renaissance in Jamaica – one that would be inclusive of the national landscape and indigenous aesthetics of the island – she took Indian cultural nationalist and poet Rabindranath Tagore as her cultural model to represent Jamaica. Marson's heightened awareness of the racial prejudice she encountered in England and her concern with women's issues served as a major cornerstone of this collection. Marson was a pioneer in illustrating how the intersections of race, gender and class contributed to the oppression that dominated the lives of African working-class women in colonial Jamaica. "The Stone Breakers" in *Moth* is one of the few poems she wrote in Jamaican Patwa and it was a commentary on the exploitative labour conditions of black working-class Jamaican women:

> Me han' hat me,
> Me back hat me,
> Me foot hat me,
> An' Lard, de sun a blin' me.

Not all of Marson's poems focused on the sorrows and suffering of black women. Coming to terms with her own African roots also meant embracing her Africanness, as exemplified in her jazz style poem "Black Is Fancy", where she unapologetically expresses love for her black self:

But now I am glad I am black,
There is something about me
That has a dash in it
Especially when I put on
My bandana.
(*Moth*, 75)

Experimentation with her jazz poems was in part a direct influence of Marson's social network that she formed with Harlem Renaissance writer James Weldon Johnson. Johnson and Marson shared a rare but special friendship even though the two never met in person. They corresponded only through letters and Johnson eventually became Marson's mentor, exposing her to the works of other Harlem Renaissance writers. (Langston Hughes was one of those writers whose contact with her was also an epistolary friendship. Hughes later published her poems in his 1949 anthology *Poetry of the Negro*.) Marson, however, "depended upon Johnson's letters, fussing about whether hers were tiresome and intrusive, worrying about letters lost or not yet answered" (*Life*, 120). Her many jazz poems in the volume included "Kinky Hair Blues", "Black Is Fancy" and "Lonesome Blues."

Obviously, Marson's colonial education still had an imprint on her. Even though many of the poems in the volume spoke candidly to racial issues, the title *The Moth and the Star* echoed Percy Shelley's "To the Moth and the Star" (1821). Her appropriation of Shelley's title, however, did not undermine the fact that Marson had at last found a distinctive Caribbean and diasporic voice that departed from the colonial influence she adhered to in her earlier volumes of poetry, which almost a decade later caused her to laugh at her juvenile effort in a letter to James Weldon Johnson in January 1938: "Tropic Reveries is so 'young' that I blush to read it." Marson's hard work of putting the collection of poems together had finally paid off and earned her more heartening responses than she had received for her earlier publications of poetry. In his introduction to the book, Philip Sherlock, co-editor of the *New Age Poetry Books* and *Caribbean Readers*, wrote,

> It has been remarked that the Blues of American Negro Literature have in them a "primitive kinship with the old ballads" and Miss Marson has made good use of the opportunities for effective repetition and for simple quick description. She has written blues which seem spontaneous rather than artificial, and that in itself is an achievement. The Blues as well as other dialect pieces are "divinations and reports" of what passes in the minds of our people.
>
> A number of poems deal . . . with the facts of race and colour. We often adopt a false attitude, and pretend that no such difference exists . . . they do exist . . . and we sometimes quite wrongly suffer injustices and insults on account of them. (*Life*, 121)

As was the case with Claude McKay's poems in Jamaican Patwa, Marson could not escape the criticism from Jamaica's elite literary circles who snubbed her use of the Jamaican language. Clare McFarlane, in a condescending review, completely dismissed the value of the Jamaican language to communicate the lived-realities of working-class African Jamaican women. For McFarlane, beauty in the artistic sense is rarely possible in a broken language; this is because the words, the materials with which the artist is building, are blurred in outline and unshapely. The materials themselves are indifferently mixed from dissimilar elements which do not always blend harmoniously. There is in the language itself something ludicrous which, while it heightens humour, often lends a farcical appearance to tragedy and makes burlesque of pathos. This is why an audience will laugh at "Stonebreakers" when it ought to feel compassion. (*Life*, 125)

Unlike her response to the barrage of criticisms that Marson received about her earlier creative work, she was unbothered by some of the disparaging comments coming from Jamaica's elite literati. She "mentally put de Lisser and McFarlane in the doghouse and looked elsewhere for advice and comfort" (*Life*, 126). Her mentor, Johnson, had already praised the collection and, besides, all that mattered to Marson was that *The Moth and the Star* finally signalled

an end to imitative art. Her cultural philosophy, which can be gleaned from several *Public Opinion* contributions, echoes James Weldon Johnson's assertion in the *Book of American Negro Poetry* (1923) that a people's greatness is recognised by one measure, above all others: "the amount and standard of literature and art they have produced". Without such obvious and contentious cultural manifestations, a people's quality and stature would remain hidden; while, on the other hand, no "people that has produced great literature and art has ever been looked upon by the world as distinctly inferior". (*Life*, 117–18)

Marson knew too well that the contemporary poets would

hardly have encouraged any digression from conventional British literary styles and themes because the "literature [in Jamaica] was really a by-product of an educational system geared to ensure loyalty to England, and designed to make us look outside for standards and values".[20]

Marson's African consciousness and challenge of the internalized anti-African racism that was inculcated through her colonial upbringing also prompted her to reassess the value of African-centred spirituality in the everyday lives of working-class African Jamaicans. This is not to say that Marson rejected her Christian faith entirely. She continued to view religion as an important phenomenon in the lives of women and, in fact, urged them to hold on to Christianity for courage. A new worldview on African/African Caribbean philosophical thinking, however, inspired her to explore African religiosity in her final play *Pocomania* (1938). Marson saw *Pocomania* or Revivalism as "the nearest thing to Africa that we have in the West Indies", it being proof that "our African ancestry is with us still" (*Life*, 136). *Pocomania* also became a part of the nationalist projects Marson sought to achieve through the literary arts. The play

> spoke directly to Jamaican indigenous religious practices. The play was certainly a turning point on what was represented on the Jamaican stage. Written in the Jamaican language, the play centralized the Africanized elements of the *pocomania* religion. This dramatic literary production also integrated and utilized Jamaican proverbs, local dance, and songs. Of equal significance were the central themes of class division and marginalisation of African cultural practices in Jamaica. Seemingly,

the play *Pocomania* pointed to a significant moment in the development of a national theatre and evoked what Marson would refer to as a "cultural renaissance".[21]

By the 1930s, despite the overwhelming Christian influence on the island, increasing number of Jamaicans were looking to their African roots for spiritual inspiration. Marson was a part of this departure from European dominant traditions. And, given the fact that the 1930s also represented the period where the valorization of black cultural aesthetics was crucial to black self-identity, African spirituality, for example, became central in the imagination of African cultural artists like Marson. Her demonstration of that retention was "an early literary attempt to reconnect Africa with the Caribbean" (*Life*, 130, 135). African-oriented movements such as Rastafari, Kumina and Pocomania all influenced a new representational atmosphere in the island and were significant in shaping the social role of the artist in Jamaica.[22] Martha Beckwith's ethnographic study, *Black Roadways: A Study of Jamaican Folk Life* (1929), of these various religious sects might have been an accessible source for Marson and other artists to draw on. Additionally, Marson would have likely observed the members of Revivalist sects, such as Pocomania, carrying out their ritual practices and would have garnered knowledge of this African-Caribbean syncretic religion in this manner.

The play *Pocomania* solidified Marson's literary reputation. She was pleased with the outcome of it and the overall reception from the public and reviewers. Philip Sherlock, for instance, commended the play as "a spirit of national consciousness" (*Life*, 136). Marson overlooked the few detractors who felt the language in the play was "uneven" and "superficial". She would turn to her mentor, Johnson, to share the joy that "Pocomania had been staged with great success". She was right to celebrate the success of her play. Marson was both realizing a national literature for her native country and extending her literary work to the African continent: "*Pocomania* had even been performed before a sympathetic Lagos audience in May 1940."[23]

In 1938, not long after the publication of *The Moth and the Star* and *Pocomania*, Marson journeyed back to England, ostensibly to raise money for Jamsave. She would remain there until 1945, the longest time she spent abroad. Her return to England was both as fruitful and as filled with disappointment as her first trip there. Marson continued on the same path in England as she had before, pursuing her writing career, continuing with her activism and developing social networks. This was the time of the Second World War, however, and a particularly lonely time for Marson. Her social life was not as vibrant as it had been in her earlier years in London. The war forced many black migrant students to move to the north of England because their universities had been evacuated, while others chose to return home. "The Negro colony in London had diminished," she wrote.[24] Despite the secluded life she now lived, and the "anxiety of having to travel alone during air-raids, lying in bed listening to doodle bombs fall" (*Life*, 155), Marson volunteered as an air-raid shelter marshal and she took on the responsibility to house people in her home during air raids until the bombing stopped.

In this tumultuous time, Marson latched onto her work at the BBC. She was first hired as a programme assistant on the Empire Service, where she would make history as the first black and West Indian woman employed in this position. Before this, Marson had done freelance work with the BBC. Marson always produced remarkable work and she devoted herself to whatever task she decided to take up. Her political commitment was to her Caribbean community and she always worked in the best interest of West Indians to legitimize their cultural presence.

Not long after she began working at the BBC, Marson and fellow Caribbean compatriot Rudolph Dunbar encouraged their BBC contacts to boost West Indians' morale in Britain and at home with Caribbean talks and programmes. Marson was promoted to work on a series with George Orwell called *Voice*, a literary show for young poets. She quickly transformed this programme into one that focused on the Caribbean, *Calling the West Indies*. This programme allowed Caribbean servicemen to send greetings back home to their family and friends. *Calling the West Indies* afforded Marson another concrete way to promote West Indian literature and culture outside of the region. Her vision of establishing a national literature included the wider anglophone Caribbean. Marson devised her own poetry programme, *Caribbean Voices*, which served as the pivotal platform to showcase Caribbean literature in the empire and the West Indies; it became "one of the most fruitful enterprises on behalf of culture in Jamaica and the West Indies".[25] Writers and would-be writers stationed in the Caribbean and England assembled in front of their radios weekly to hear the well-known opening greeting: "Hello this is London Calling the West Indies." Established literary names such as George Lamming, V.S. Naipaul and Samuel Selvon were among the many authors who used *Caribbean Voices* as a platform to feature their work. Years after the programme came to an end, Marson would express delight in fulfilling her poetic vision of Caribbean regionalism when she states, "during the war years, I introduced the programme called Caribbean Voices and invited all West Indian writers to contribute. BBC standards are high, but through the years the programme has been maintained and has provided an inspiring outlet for our writings" (*Life*, 159).

West Indian literature as a whole owes thanks to a forward-thinking regionalist like Marson. The "program's importance in establishing a Caribbean literary presence and in creating a network of writers on both sides of the Atlantic cannot be underestimated and is often stressed, but rarely is Marson's name mentioned".[26] What seems to also be forgotten is that "the overwhelming majority of her work at the corporation involved producing and compering 'variety'-style entertainment programs that entailed forms of collective rather than individual expression and therefore were expected to be equitable and representative rather than autonomous or idiosyncratic".[27]

While Marson's work with the BBC was to be her most rewarding and constructive creation, in 1945, she got the impulse to leave London's cold weather, motivated in part by the fatigue of the war, "but more than anything else", she felt the urge "to come to the West Indies to meet as many people as possible" to whom she "had been speaking for nearly five years" (*Life*, 169). Marson toured various Caribbean islands for some months to get away from the stress of England. Her first stop in Jamaica gave her a completely different welcome than she had received on her first trip home from England. On this return, Marson's reception was like that of a celebrity. "Everywhere she went, huge crowds gathered as though she were royalty" (*Life*, 169). There were speeches commending Marson's work and her impact on local literature. Her name appeared in the newspaper just about every day with reports of functions she attended. Marson was also warmly welcomed in the other Caribbean islands that she visited.

Marson's return to the BBC in 1945 was a short tenure. Personal and professional tensions, her usual overwork, travel stints and dissatisfaction with the world all began to take a toll on her, which resulted in another emotional breakdown. Besides being overworked at the BBC, records show that Marson's short-lived experience with *Caribbean Voices* resulted from niggling racial intolerance she experienced from her colleagues. A private document on Marson's work performance during a BBC training course revealed that, though mostly positive, she had to contend with the "social" difficulties of "prejudice which undoubtedly exist among some of the staff". The BBC granted Marson sick leave, so that she could benefit from what one manager called "her home environment".[28] She eventually returned to Jamaica with the financial help of J.E. Clare McFarlane. This time she retreated into isolation for nearly two years. Marson had taken so much time and trouble over the job, the tour and her research and it all had come to nothing. She felt the influence of an unjust world that told her she could hold on no longer. About a month after her return to Kingston, Una was admitted to Bellevue Mental Hospital for rest and observation. This was a time of relief and release from all her pain. The anger and resentment which she had stored from her years in England, the ambivalent feelings about her parents long dead and her fear about her own uncertain future, engulfed her. (*Life*, 175–76)

Marson's road to full recovery was filled with its ups and downs. There were long periods of silence in her writing followed by outbursts of activity. Marson's illness had caused her to miss Langston Hughes's visit to Jamaica in October 1947. This she deeply regretted, given their regular correspondence during the key points of her writing career and his influence on her work. Hughes's visit to the island came at a time when black literature was making its mark: departing from a Western-European literary style, it celebrated African cultures in the Americas. This would mark the second time Marson missed the chance to meet with Langston Hughes, the first being in London. On that occasion, however, Marson's friend Vivian Virtue was able to pass on a few of her poems, which were later published in Hughes's anthology. While the two poems selected for the anthology did not entirely reflect Marson's modes of writing, particularly the ones that spoke to her black internationalism, she was still grateful for the opportunity to have her poetry exposed to an American audience. Twenty years after her death, Marson's poetic quality and range were generously featured in the *Penguin Book of Caribbean Verse in English* (1986), compiled by Paula Burnett. Ironically, then, it was Britain, the country she was always at odds with, that eventually "assured her [a] place in the West Indian literary canon" by way of that publication (*Life*, 184).

The Jamaican landscape provided Marson with the peace of mind she sought after her institutionalization. She toured various parts of the country as she rediscovered the landscape she had left behind and she treated herself to the unexplored countryside. Finding temporary comfort also in her family and friends, her health was restored and, in no time, she became the general editor for the Pioneer Press, which had been established as the book publishing department of the Gleaner Company Limited (publishers of Jamaica's daily newspaper). She had finally realized her long-term goal of a publishing endeavour intended to bring out inexpensive editions of works by Jamaican authors. Several books came out of this press, including Marson's own poems that she had contributed to *Anancy Stories and Dialect Verse* by Louise Bennett. Marson's free time from the press was spent trying to strengthen Jamaica's literary scene, devoting her time to upcoming writers, and to Readers and Writers Club she had formed years earlier.

Andrew Salkey was one of the writers who benefited from Marson's generosity when her literary focus turned to her native country in 1949. Years after her death, Salkey took the time to acknowledge that Marson was

> very generous, gracious and supportive, always finding ample
> time, in her very busy schedule, as a journalist at the *Daily*

> *Gleaner* and as an unpaid, island-wide, crusading cultural
> worker, to read our manuscripts, and offer us excellent critical
> comment and encouragement. . . . She was a splendid example
> of the writer who had made a reputation abroad and yet who
> was willing to help us with our poems, stories, plays, essays and
> newspaper articles. (*Life*, 182)

Even though Marson's dream of working for a broadcasting company in the Caribbean was never fulfilled, the contact she maintained with the BBC helped to cushion her disappointment. Marson's physical absence from the broadcasting company did not deter her from promoting Caribbean literature. She continued to make her presence felt at the BBC. She pushed for Jamaican representation on the radio and she also wrote to Henry Swanzy, who had taken charge of *Caribbean Voices*, to encourage him to include Jamaican works on her old radio programme. Marson kept up her aggressive campaign for a national literature in the local media as well. In a provocative article in the *Sunday Gleaner* (23 October 1949), Marson considered the status of writers and literature in Jamaica in comparison to writers and literature in other territories. Writers were not encouraged in her island, she wrote, and they were even ridiculed. As she candidly highlighted, "the truth is that it has not yet come to the hearts and minds of the people of this island that our status in the way of nationhood is more to be enhanced by our literary input than by rum and bananas". Noting the lack of financial support available to Jamaican writers, she commented, "our writers have no Guggenheim, Rockefeller or Rosenwald Scholarship to keep them". Indeed, Marson championed views that were not often vocalized at the time but have become openly contested in the decades since.

Though she was able to achieve a great number of her goals, with reference to the development of a literary culture, Marson became dissatisfied with the direction her country was heading. In her article "What's Wrong with Jamaica?", she voiced her frustration at the Americanization of sections of the population whose "eyes and thoughts [were] directed away from Jamaica" (*Life*, 192). Another piece expressed her concerns about the impact American cinema had on the youth, a discussion that has not left the Jamaican public discourse until this day. The Alexander Bustamante–led government that came to power with the introduction of universal adult suffrage and internal self-government in 1944 seemed to have been a failure in Marson's eyes. In keeping with her usual response to life's disappointments, Marson once again packed up and exited Jamaica's literary scene and the country altogether. England had offered Marson little to no refuge in her times of anguish so on her final expatriation from Jamaica, ironically, she turned to the United States, the country she was highly critical of for its influence on the Jamaican populace. This was also the country she had avoided going to in the earlier periods of her career.

Marson's eight-year stay in the United States did not offer better treatment than the hostility of the imperial metropolis. She had expected more freedom in the United States, but the institutionalized racism she encountered, a racist policy she had not experienced in England, was a culture shock for her. Not even in Jamaica, where the colour bar was rigidly in place, did this discrimination come close to the apartheid system that she encountered in the United States. In Miami, she visited public places that were forbidden to her. Characteristically, she paid no attention to such prohibitions and wrote defiantly of her rebelliousness: "We had been warned that we could not walk into a place in downtown Miami and have a cool drink. Well, we did and nothing happened and we enjoyed it." She wrote about her tearful humiliation of being refused service in an Italian restaurant as well as being denied admission to two movie theatres. Marson bitterly described also how she was "served" in a drug store: she was given a cup of tea in a cardboard container wrapped in a paper bag. "How on earth," she questioned, "can coloured people live in a place [where] they are treated on account of their colour? What does it do to them?" Marson became even more disturbed at the idea of racially segregated churches, which she saw as a "contradiction in terms".[29] Although Marson would have been aware of the plight of African Americans through essays and fictional works of her Harlem Renaissance literary acquaintances, the fact of her not being able to experience the vibrancy of the Harlem Renaissance might have, to some degree, contributed to the disappointment she felt during her temporary residency in the United States.

Marson eventually settled in Washington, DC, and continued to do her journalistic work, but no major developments have been linked to her time spent there. She used this period to go back to school; she attended evening classes at the local universities and took writing courses in television, theatre and children's literature. Her attempts at writing children's stories were occasionally successful, with a few of her pieces being published. "Christmas on Poinsettia Island", a short story set in Jamaica appeared in *American Junior Red Cross*. Her other writings included unpublished articles where she reported her observations of American life and her experiences of segregation.

In 1960, at age fifty-five, Marson was married for a few months to an African American dentist, Peter Staples, a widower with two adult daughters. After the separation from her husband, Marson fell into a depression and was hospitalized in Washington, DC, by the Staples family before returning to Jamaica. Her mental breakdown was said to have been triggered by "her own 'dissatisfaction with life'" which "was probably now of a sexual nature. With the desires and needs between husband and wife neither understood nor met, so much was probably being repressed. The marriage itself was a closely guarded secret even among Marson's closer friends and associates in Jamaica. Some people have suggested that Peter Staples required a stabilising influence from his second wife: Una could not, or perhaps would not, accommodate his needs" (*Life*, 204–5).

Back in Jamaica, just in time for the island's independence in 1962, Marson's social work became her focus. She re-joined Jamsave, which she had left in its early stage of development in 1938. Significantly, at this period, she also got involved in the struggles of the Rastafari community. Marson had spent half of her life challenging all forms of oppression, including her efforts to liberate Jamaica from European education that deemed African culture to be inferior. Her support for the

Rastafari community would have stemmed from her experience fighting against the Fascist takeover of Ethiopia and her time spent with His Imperial Majesty Haile Selassie. Ethiopia represented home for Rastafari and Selassie was their Christlike figure. Advocating for the Rasta community is perhaps one of the most courageous steps Marson took on throughout her career, given the brutal attacks and discrimination the group faced. Aligning herself with a rebellious and outcast group would have been a huge departure from her colonial upbringing. Nonetheless, she was able to establish the Foreshore Road Infant Centre for Rastafarian Children. Marson's involvement in supporting the rights of Rastafari was far from politically motivated. And she was not afraid to criticize intellectuals she thought too scholarly in their approach and not proactive or practical. In response to university research on the Rastafarian movement, she openly chastised researchers on what she saw as their lame effort to champion the Rastafarian cause: "I must say I find myself getting a bit impatient with people who need to research for seven months to find out what is obvious. I suppose getting to know the area and winning people over is important but when one starts with the knowledge of urgent needs, the planning and persuasion should not be too long drawn out" (*Life*, 209). Marson's criticism of the university researchers was misplaced, given the fact that the 1960 *Report on Ras Tafari Movement in Kingston, Jamaica* was completed within two weeks after carrying out intensive in the field interviews and observation of the Rastafari community in the capital city. Marson, out of frustration, possibly conflated the slow response of the government to implement the report's recommendations with the actual completion of the document itself. Negotiations of the terms outlined in the report dragged on for two years after its release with only some of the recommendations being fully met.[30]

As Jamaica celebrated its independence, Marson raised questions. Surely, she must have been happy to have lived to finally witness Jamaica become an independent state. She had aggressively campaigned for this in her own call for a national literature and cultural renaissance. However, she was disappointed that the People's National Party, Norman Manley's party, lost the general election. Therefore, her concern was the issue of what national leadership and independence really meant. "It would be a long time before all the people of this young nation will fully understand and succeed in living up to the implications of independence" ("The Foundation of Independence", *Daily Gleaner*, 1 August 1964). Also, although the country had got its independence, Marson found its narrow cultural horizon frustrating. To make matters worse, Clare McFarlane's *A Literature in the Making* (1956) did not include Louise Bennett's Patwa poems, which was completely in opposition to all that Marson had worked to accomplish both in Jamaica and overseas. Her health issues, her high blood pressure and weight gain did not make life any easier for her as she struggled to advance her country's pride and dignity.

Two years after independence, Marson's work with Jamsave resulted in a trip to Israel when she received an invitation to attend a three-day seminar for women leaders.

Though Marson was fifty-nine years old, Aaron Matalon, a prominent local businessman who was also the Israeli honorary consul in Jamaica, thought her enthusiasm was best suited for the task. Matalon was also aware of Marson's impressive work with women's issues and saw her as the perfect candidate to carry out the work, irrespective of her political affiliation. Her trip to Israel was successful. Before returning to Jamaica, she used some of her time to stop over in London to visit her old friends. Of course, many changes had taken place. There was an established West Indian immigrant community that had also come to England in search of a better life and, what pleased her most, was the growing literary community of young Caribbean writers and artists.

Marson was content to see that the new generation of writers were "less patient" with European domination and that they continued the struggle for cultural visibility in British society. This was the generation who had benefited from *Caribbean Voices* and they were the proud intellects of the newly independent Caribbean nations. She made sure to take advantage of the energy among these enthusiastic poets and novelists. She did her last literary engagement with the BBC, which included a recorded interview with her mentee Andrew Salkey, and she happily met with George Lamming and other writers. Marson's last radio broadcast with the BBC, however, was on the flagship programme *Woman's Hour*, where she discussed her trip to Israel.

Fearing to return to little or nothing in Jamaica, Marson went back to Israel to complete a three-month contract. She would unknowingly be given her last work assignment when she was awarded a British Council scholarship to do research on social development in Jamaica. But depression hit her at the thought of returning to Jamaica. For the first time, Marson felt her native home could no longer provide refuge. There appeared to be no place for Marson in her own Jamaican society. After being persuaded to return to Jamaica by a friend, a dejected Marson journeyed back in a state of depression. When she arrived in Jamaica, she suffered a series of heart attacks and died ten days later.

Una Marson died on 6 May 1965 and was buried at Saint Andrew Parish Church on 10 May. The officiating Reverend Carnegie reminded a packed church of the rich and incredible life Marson had lived. From a small rural community, a colonial school girl became a world traveller. She experienced a wide range of cultures and remained devoted to the cultural progression of her race, the advancement of women and the national development of her country of birth. These were the core values of Marson's work.

Most significantly, Marson wisely recognized that "one is shaped by one's travels and that one also shapes one's travels",[31] which she expressed in "Discovering America":

> It is impossible to approach a country absolutely objectively. We all carry with us something of what we have seen and lived and loved. It is bound to colour what we see in a new country. . . . I carried the quiet of the mountains, the dignity and poise of my country's people and the peace of gentle waves lapping the white sands on the shores of a moonlit tropical night.

THREE

Marson's literary work – her fictional characters, blended with personal experiences and political events – offers insights into her life. Her first collection of poetry, *Tropic Reveries* (1930), offered the reader a glimpse of her lonely life, one filled with the possible loss of, and disappointments in, her own romantic relationships. These are some of the central themes that permeate the collection. The image of an abandoned woman overcome with grief or a woman longing for love is recurrently suggested; in just about every poem, the speaker fantasizes about vanished love, wishes to die or feels depressed. For Marson, love and grief were "twin souls". As the lonesome woman experiences an array of emotions, she resigns herself to the bittersweet nature of being in love. Accordingly, the grieving lonely woman sometimes expresses jealousy:

> I know too well beloved
> That thou art not for me
> That other hands and other hearts
> Will minister to thee.

I know those eyes so tender
On others still will shine
And that your kiss will linger
On other lips than mine.
(*Tropic*, 49)

Or sometimes the melancholic woman simply yearns to be loved and desired: "Play bridge! when each fibre of my aching heart / Yearned just for the touch of your hand" (*Heights*, 43).

While Marson was still struggling to find her literary voice and style in this collection, her feminist politics had already been shaped and would take precedence in her poems. Aside from the lonely damsel in distress in the love poetry, there is an open attack on marriage.

In "To Wed or Not to Wed", Marson questions the conventional ideas of heterosexual marriage as the instinctive choice for women in 1930s Jamaica. She scoffs at marriage as a forced middle-class ideal for women. There are many reasons for this. One was that many Jamaican men turned down their darker-skinned counterparts for lighter-skinned partners in order to gain status in an anti-African, racist and colonized Jamaican society. Rhonda Cobham explains:

> Social studies of Jamaican middle-class society between the wars and after draw attention to the disproportionate number of unmarried black women within the Jamaican middle-class. They attribute this to the tendency of Jamaican men to marry upward on the colour scale, rejecting well-educated women of their own shade or darker in preference to fairer-complexioned women or foreign white women through whom they could increase their social prestige in Jamaican circles.[32]

Similarly, in her poem "If", she critiques patriarchy when she parodies Rudyard Kipling's poem of the same name and goes against matrimony. In the poem, Marson chastises the oppressive nature of housewifery, and names the sacrifices women are forced to make to achieve their duties as wives when she states:

> If you can make him spend the evenings with you
> When fifty Jims and Jacks are on his mind
> . . . if you can bear to hear the truth you tell him
> Twisted around to make you seem a fool.
> (*Tropic*, 83)

In the conclusion of the poem, she maintains that these and other sacrifices can be made so that "you'll be a wife worthwhile". Marson's poem revealed the realities of an idealized romance that is often projected within a patriarchal structure, bringing attention to the inequality in the expectations of a woman's role in heterosexual marriage.

Marson continued to focus on emotionally distraught individuals in her second collection of poems, *Heights and Depths* (1931). The lonely woman persona once again dominates the pages. The poems also reveal how Marson had become socially conscious of the environment in which she lived and her interest in the realities of how women lived. In "A Dream", for example, the speaker desires death. In the poem "Love's Eclipse", she employs the metaphors of the sun and the moon to talk about her unhappiness at having been deserted:

That darkness such as comes before the morn
Would seem as light to that which came to me
When thus you left me lonely and forlorn.
(*Heights*, 49)

Marson was twenty-six when *Heights and Depths* was published and the love themes she explored in the collection as
well as in *Tropic Reveries* raised questions about her virginity
and sexuality. The characters in *Tropic Reveries* (1930) and
Heights and Depths (1931) unfortunately engaged readers in
"a wild goose chase after male lovers, not only because their
identities matter less than the inner world of the woman herself but also because emotional involvement with women was
the more vital force in her life. Her bond with Ethel and later
friendships with feminist women abroad provided the source
from which Una was able to grow a positive self-definition.
There is, however, no evidence of a lesbian relationship in the
accepted sense" (*Life*, 42–43).

Her third volume of poetry, *The Moth and the Star*, represents a more confident woman. When literary critic Lloyd
Brown comments that the volume "reflects Marson's maturity
after migrating to England",[33] he has taken notice of the major
distinction between her first two collections and the third.
These poems were influenced by Marson's time spent away
from her native country, Jamaica. Marson's experience in the
mother country had deepened her awareness from many
angles: she became more conscious of being a West Indian
and she was no longer chained to the notion of being a British
subject. Marson also gained a refined awareness of nationalism and what it meant for a country to be an independent

nation. As well, her marginalization in her new home, as a black person and as a woman, helped to form the themes addressed in *The Moth and the Star*.

The Moth and the Star speaks explicitly to the alienation Marson encountered in England. "Little Brown Girl" is just another instance in which Marson highlights the alienation she endured. This racial harassment is subtler than the name calling blurted out in the polemic "Nigger", which had been published in the *Keys,* the newsletter of the League of Coloured Peoples. "Little Brown Girl" depicts an unnamed black woman, likely Marson herself, who is being bombarded with questions by a white Londoner. The Londoner asks,

> Why do you wander alone
> . . . .
> Why do you start and wince
> When white folk stare at you?
> (*Moth*, 11)

Throughout the poem, the white speaker directs rambling questions at Marson's racialized gaze and creates a sense of "intimidation and alienation". "Little Brown Girl" touchingly describes black British life in general for the colonized migrants and, particularly, the way Marson negotiated her cultural outsider/insider status in London. The poem was originally called "Autobiography of a Brown Girl", a title evocative of James Weldon Johnson's classic, *The Autobiography of an Ex-Colored Man* (1912). Marson admired this classic and she saw in it parallels with her own life as a black British woman. It is a great shame that Marson's own autobiography was never found, for that would provide a rich view of the black colonial migrant's reality in pre-war and wartime London that would round out the post-war experience so vividly captured by Sam Selvon in *The Lonely Londoners* (1956) and George Lamming in *The Emigrants* (1954).

Marson's efforts to establish a national literature strengthened as she came to understand the importance of a country's literature. This need for a cultural renaissance would have become apparent to Marson because of her own colonial education that valorized European literature. In England, Marson would have observed first-hand the pride that England took in her literature and culture and understood the need for African Jamaicans to begin telling their own narratives in imaginative ways. In the *Public Opinion* article "Readers and Writers Club" (31 July 1937), she echoes Marcus Garvey's call to black people to tell their own stories: "For many decades European writers have been revealing the mind of the Negro to Europeans. Now the Negro is becoming articulate. It is important that he should become more so – that he should have a clear idea of what he thinks and what he wants. These ideas must be expressed so that they can be widely read" (*Life*, 117).

Marson's personal journey expressed in *The Moth and the Star* also shows an appreciation of black cultures of Jamaica, the culture that was devalued in favour of Britishness. What better way to express the indigenized culture than through the language of the people? Four of the poems published in the collection are written in Jamaican Patwa. Despite the unpopularity of the vernacular in literature in general at that time, Marson relied on the local language to tell the stories of the everyday lives of working-class Jamaicans. "The Stone Breakers", for instance, authentically speaks of the exploitation of black people at the hands of the white colonials, who, in the end, are the beneficiaries of their hard labour: "De big backra car dem / A lik up de dus' in a we face" (*Moth*, 70).

Marson's use of the local language is groundbreaking for this period and it is given even greater weight when she allows her character to speak Jamaican beyond the shores of his home. "Quashie Comes to London", also from the poems written in England, gives us an insight into a homesick African Caribbean migrant who wanders the cold streets of London, longing for the warmth of his homeland. The persona also uses this time to lament his loneliness. Unlike the "Little Brown Girl", Quashie confidently speaks for himself using his own nation language when he states:

> An' sometimes jes when I feel gran'
> Dere sitting all alone,
> Dem play some tune dat takes me home
> In sweet and soulful tone,
>
> An' de tears dem well up in me eyes
> An' I try fe brush dem 'way,
> But me heart gets full and dough I try
> Dem simply come fe stay.
> (*Moth*, 18)

"Quashie Comes to London" also reintroduces a diasporic sensibility that becomes a major feature in Caribbean literature: the expatriate's longing for home and offering commentary on the adopted country. In this way, "Quashie embodies a country bumpkin archetype who makes the transformative journey of emigration to the metropolis".[34] Quashie's home-sickness is also demonstrated in Marson's references to food. Here, Marson lists the names of Jamaican foods to comment further on the migrant's longing for home. Quashie enters a restaurant and tries to order a cuisine alien to the British diet:

> . . . "Some ripe breadfruit,
> Some fresh ackee and saltfish too
> An' dumplins hot will suit."

When Quashie learns that he is unable to indulge in his native food, he resorts to ordering anything, commenting,

> It's den me miss me home sweet home
> Me good ole rice an' peas
> An' I say I is a fool fe come
> To dis lan' of starve an' sneeze.
> (*Moth*, 20–21)

In contrast to Marson's other poems that are based on her personal experience, Quashie speaks collectively and directly to the Caribbean migrant's response to the metropolis, irrespective of the class of the people – country bumpkin or not.

Very similar to Claude McKay's *Songs of Jamaica* (1912) and *Constab Ballads* (1912) that capture the natural landscape of the island, Marson also showcases the geographical landscape of Jamaica in *The Moth and the Star*, in contrast to the romanticized British nature poems she wrote for her first two collections. Where many of the literary works of this period focused on capturing the British scenery, "Mango Time Again", for example, explores the landscape and emotions associated with mango season:

> Not gwine hungry anymore
> Mango start fe ripe,
> Not gwine stay inside me door
> Mango start fe ripe.
> (*Moth*, 86)

Influenced by Garvey, Marson's support of African cultural expressions was intended to be a vehicle to challenge white cultural hegemony and was also to be seen as a connecting force to unite African people and to ignite African pride. As the dialogue among the Black Atlantic cultures emerged, black literature became critical for Marson's break from her colonial literary forms. Therefore, the inclusion of jazz poetry in *The Moth and the Star* was no accident. "The new musical, jazzy poets stirred her and she dreamt of catching, Caribbean-style, something of this innovative black verve. From time to time she heard more of what was going on in Harlem, admired it and wanted to be in contact with the Harlem Renaissance writers. A steady stream of black artists was trickling into Britain. They brought jazz, they brought blues" (*Life*, 84). In addition to her preferred musical taste, the African American vernacular blended with her own cultural traditions and became the central literary aesthetic for Marson's blues poetry. These blues poems would voice Marson's love and difficulties, and an African woman's identity.

Having grown up in a society where colourism prevailed,

Marson carried the weight of being a dark-skinned woman and "was deeply unhappy because as a dark-skinned scholarship girl she was made to feel inadequate and unacceptable by the posh majority who knew and enjoyed the privilege of 'whiteness': 'Let it be said also that the 20 or so really dark girls were snubbed by some white and near white girls' " (*Life*, 19). Her series of black self-affirmation poems, some of which were influenced by jazz, would, therefore, speak unwaveringly to what can be interpreted as Marson's anxieties about herself and about her renewed self-confidence. In his introduction to the collection, Philip Sherlock pointed to the "quieter assumption" of her group identity and heritage (*Moth*, xii). In the poem "Black Is Fancy," the female narrator ventriloquizes Marson's own voice and declares,

> I used to feel
> I was so ugly,
> Because I am black,
> But now I am glad I am black.
> (*Moth*, 75)

Marson's experience in England also took her back to how colour prejudice negatively impacted black women's self-esteem, a topic that she had written about in the *Cosmopolitan*, after the Miss Jamaica beauty pageant. Marson's confidence in wearing her hair natural and embracing an African aesthetic both in fashion style and culture is articulated in her poems, such as "Kinky Hair Blues". In this poem, Marson rejects processed hair as she objects to falling prey to the white beauty myth:

Gwine find a beauty shop
Cause I aint a lovely belle.
The boys pass me by,
They say I's not so swell.

See oder young gals
So slick and smart.
. . . .
I jes gwine die on de shelf
If I don't mek a start.

I hate dat ironed hair
And dat bleaching skin.
. . . .
But I'll be all alone
If I don't fall in.
(*Moth*, 91)

Also heard in the speaker's voice is Marson's own concern about the rejection she possibly encountered from men as a result of her choice to wear her hair natural and skin unbleached. Marson refused to compromise her black self-love for ideals of beauty that privileged whiteness. Her feelings expressed here are perhaps telling of her personal relationships with men as discussed in her earlier work.

Lord 'tis you did gie me
All dis kinky hair.
. . . .
And I don't envy gals
What got dose locks so fair.

I like me black face

And me kinky hair.
. . . .
But nobody loves dem,
I jes don't tink it's fair.

Now I's gwine press me hair
And bleach me skin.
. . . .
What won't a gal do
Some kind a man to win.
(*Moth*, 91)

The collection also signalled Marson's commitment to caution a younger generation of black women against being influenced by dominant white images in the media. In "Cinema Eyes", a mother discourages her child from going to a cinema until "black beauties / Are chosen for the screen" (*Moth*, 88). Marson recounts her own history as a warning to the "cinema mind" that led to her rejection of blackness and adoration for the white celebrities whom she saw on screen.

The Moth and the Star encapsulates Marson's real-life struggle against her critics in that she no longer sought the approval of Jamaica's literary circle. In this way, the collection confirmed Marson's final push to find her own poetic voice and style, a voice that no longer mimicked her colonial education or sang praises of empire. This voice allowed Marson to create more writings that revealed her personal growth as a writer and the love she had for her race and nation, themes that are also forcefully addressed in some of her plays.

Marson's dramatic works, like her poems, change over time from closely biographical to openly political. *At What a*

Price (1932) perhaps marks the beginning of Marson's attempt to depart from traditional British literature. This was her first play and was co-authored with Horace Vaz, but it was mainly Marson's work. Vaz was a friend from Jamaica who had also moved to London. The play was first performed at the Ward Theatre in Kingston, Jamaica, and was staged later in London, becoming the first black colonial production in the West End. In line with Marson's desire to develop a national literature, the play satisfied all the criteria for a truly Jamaican play: it was written by a Jamaican, about Jamaican subjects and performed with Jamaican actors.

While this play does not chronicle Marson's early life, the protagonist similarly embarks on a journey from country to town and Marson's social views are reflected in the development of the plot. Marson subtly depicts the dangers of having to leave the security of one's family (and boyfriend, Robert) and a safe environment, and "her conclusion is that even though we pay a high price for our worldly education, the price is worth it".[35] In the play, Marson is also starting to contemplate the world outside of rural Jamaica. The main character, Ruth Maitland, is a girl from the country who comes to the city to take up a clerical job, as Marson had done. She later becomes pregnant for her lighter-skinned employer. Marson uses this relationship between Ruth and her employer to present the class and colour prejudice found in Jamaica. For example, when Ruth reads a letter from her poor relative, her middle-class manager ridicules the dialect. By this time in her life, Marson is well aware of the middle-class snobbery toward Jamaican Patwa, a way of speaking that she champions in her plays to valorize African Jamaican folk culture.

Marson's understanding of the deeply embedded colour prejudice in Jamaica is shown in Ruth's refusal to marry her boss, stating, "I told him he offered me marriage because he thought he wrong me . . . in time he would only remember that I, his wife, was not of his colour . . . he would hate me" (act 4, scene 2). Because there is little information known about Marson's romantic affairs, it is difficult to know if she shared Ruth's feeling about dating and mating with lighter-skinned or white men of higher social status since she was perhaps privately hiding her fear of being rejected. Archie Lindo, an admirer of Marson, had openly suggested in an interview that he always thought that Una was saving herself for a white man (*Life*, 40).

Marson's preoccupation with interracial dating had been revealed earlier in her short story "Sojourn", written for the *Cosmopolitan* in 1931. Helen, the main character, a dark-complexioned Jamaican woman, falls in love with an Englishman, Sidney. Helen is portrayed as being overly sensitive and self-conscious about her colour, but Sidney is oblivious to it. Helen eventually realizes that Sidney genuinely loves her and sheds the self-imposed barriers between them. The relationship does not develop because Sidney has to suddenly return to England and Helen is left to wonder whether their relationship would have had the chance to grow. Marson's personal concerns with interracial courting is justifiably portrayed in her work of fiction because she herself "confronted the fact that men did not find her beautiful. Although she counted many men among her acquaintances, several have commented negatively about her physical appearance: 'In those days the emphasis we placed on beauty and form was different'" (*Life*, 41). Marson's early work is symptomatic of her initial gullibility about race relations in colonial Jamaica and her idealized view of these attitudes in "Sojourn" would be drastically transformed almost a decade later.

In *At What a Price*, Marson revisits her feminist sensibilities. This play can be read as Marson's position on marriage and women's agency in relationships. First, Ruth is not described as the exemplary romantic heroine; instead, she is portrayed as an independent and assertive woman. Ruth rejects the marriage proposal of her boss because of her moral upbringing. Before Ruth returns to the city, she exhibits an overtly feminist position. Ruth admonishes her boyfriend when she says, "Don't you dare to be so absolutely Victorian as to tell me the woman's place is in the home" (act 1, scene 1). Ruth embodies the independence, ambition and unconventional ways of Marson as she challenges traditional gender roles. Ruth also echoes Marson's own opposition to the conventions of marriage revealed in her poems "To Wed" and "If". However, Ruth, unlike Marson, originates from a working-class background. Parallel to the female protagonists in Marson's poems written in Jamaican Patwa, Ruth is far from the deserted, wounded woman who longs to be loved. She represents the rural folk. In the poem "The Stone Breakers", for instance, the women moan about their worthless husbands, among other things. "In Marson's mind, it seems the sort of woman who speaks dialect" (or, I add, who comes from the labouring class) "would not pine for her lost love like the personae of her other poems".[36] However, Marson's sympathy for working-class women's experience of "lost love" may stem from her own feelings of alienation from the middle-class because of the colour prejudice she faced both as a child and an adult.

Moreover, throughout her creative works, Marson introduces us to women who, like herself, are regarded by society to be sexually undesirable by men because they are too dark-skinned. Ruth does not consider herself to be physically attractive; as she states, "I am not beautiful enough to be ornamental" (act 1, scene 1).

Outside of its fictional world, *At What a Price* nudges at Marson's steady growth as a writer. Horace Vaz later commended Una as a pioneer who had valorized the use of Jamaican themes, characters, and settings. She also received nods from critics at the *Daily Gleaner* (13 June 1932) who called for "more such productions and greater public support for local writers". Marson was becoming more confident as a Jamaican playwright and she saw the need to evaluate British dominance in Jamaican theatre in terms of language, themes and attitudes, and she continued to nativize her later plays by drawing on African Jamaican culture as the main source of her literary content.

London Calling (1937), Marson's second play, is another fictional piece that provides insight into her political views and into facets of her personal life. Although the play was comedic, Marson did not hesitate to touch on the serious political climate of the time. She began writing the play shortly after the departure from London of Ofori Atta, an African chief and possibly a romantic partner of hers. The plot, as in Marson's first play, echoes her journey away from home, a motif that frames all of her plays. In short, *London Calling* tells the story of colonial migrants who travelled from a fictional country, Novokan, to London, and of their friend, Prince Altoa, from Africa. The imaginary Novokan is said to be based on Marson's knowledge of Akyem Abuakwa, in the Eastern region of Ghana, of which the chief spoke highly (*Life*, 70). Also, the character Prince Altoa was inspired by Ofori Atta. The central themes explore how black colonial students in London responded to British stereotypes of Africans and Caribbean people. The students invited to the Burtons, a British family that had racial stereotypes of African people, take pleasure in ridiculing the family through over-dramatizing colonial typecasts of Africans and characterizing African Caribbean people as uncivilized.

Even though the play was dismissed as "basically a romantic comedy" with no social relevance,[37] one can obviously draw parallels between Marson's fictional black students and the educated black migrants she surrounded herself with daily. The relevance of the social issues Marson incorporated into the play is very much evident. The students, similar to real-life black intellectuals and activists, struggle with issues such as interracial dating, racial discrimination, migration, homesickness and other topical issues affecting colonial migrants. Marson's strong political consciousness is plainly articulated throughout the play. For instance, Altoa's comments that he is taking the Burtons "back to Africa" by dressing them up in colourful African clothing and beads and teaching them dance steps is a clear nod in the direction of Garveyism and pan-African politics.

Marson's time spent with Ofori Atta during his visit to England can be said to have inspired *London Calling*. Marson, as a representative of the League of Coloured Peoples, was assigned to Atta and the two spent much time together discussing, at great length, African politics. This relationship inspired what Jarrett-Macauley describes as a "change in political consciousness" on Marson's part (*Life*, 73). This influence pushed Marson to not only develop an African consciousness, politically, but motivated her to research African history and culture, read African literary works, and form friendships with African activists such as Lapido Solanke, founder of the West African Students' Union. All of this new knowledge and admiration for Mother Africa was crystallized in *London Calling*.

Pocomania (1937), Marson's last play, dramatizes her ultimate journey to self-awareness, cultural discovery, and the intersection of her pan-Africanist politics and black feminism. Written in the same year as *The Moth and the Star*, *Pocomania* would also be the play that confirmed Marson's status as a playwright and it finally legitimized African Jamaican culture through theatrical form. Filled with the celebration of African drums, dance, worship and Jamaican Patwa, *Pocomania* was a milestone in the development of a national Jamaican theatre. The play explored Marson's need to escape the constraints of colonial ideals in order to better understand herself as a black middle-class woman. Stella Manners, the

protagonist, is the daughter of a pastor who wishes to escape
the dull rural lifestyle she had lived as a child: "I am sick to
death of the quietness here," she complains (act 1, scene 2).
Stella's longing for an adventurous life contrasts with the life
of her contented sister, Dawn, a character who may be based
on Marson's sisters, Edith and Ethel, who settled for conventional lives. For Stella, Pocomania becomes a site of healing
after the death of her childhood sweetheart. In a sense, her
embrace of the religion is a search for cultural belonging,
given the fact that she was detached from working-class folk
culture. Stella is guided by her spiritual mother, the Revivalist
Sister Kate, to understand the true meaning and value of the
religious practices of Pocomania or Pukkumina. Sister Kate's
guidance also helps counter the negative connotations associated with Pocomania and lauds the religion as an example
of Jamaica's African roots:

> **Stella**: I don't know whether I like them [the drums] or not.
> They frighten me a little but they certainly fascinate me.
>
> **Sister Kate**: Fascinate, Miss Stella? Dem is more wonderful dan
> dat! Troo de drum de spirit speaks – de Lawd Himself speak to
> de soul of people.
> (Act 1, scene 2)

Pocomania indirectly featured central figures in Marson's
life: "Ada Marson had so emotionally absented herself from
her daughter's life that Una felt like a motherless child. In her
plays mothers are either dead or weak" (*Life*, 9). In *Pocomania*, Stella's mother is dead and she seeks an alternative
mother figure in Sister Kate. Sister Kate might, in some ways,

represent Cousin Angie, who for Marson filled the void left by her mother's emotional distance. The play could be read as an artistic protest against middle-class Jamaican or Afro-Saxon culture and as a critique of Marson's own upbringing. Stella's first-hand contact with Pocomania goes against colonial middle-class religious values, and her father, the local parson, opposes her fascination with it.

The play ends with Stella returning to her own class and religion, and she eventually marries. The character of Stella contrasts with that of Ruth Maitland, who refuses marriage in *At What a Price*. Even though Stella succumbs to convention, the ending does not invalidate Marson's attempt to wrestle with the complexities of a middle-class woman's desire for freedom. Pragmatically, the social reality of the early twentieth century would not grant a young middle-class woman such freedom. Women who dared to violate class barriers and sexual conventions were considered deviant and treated as insane. Stella Manners is "a creative, expressive soul . . . [an] ambitious but trapped New Woman. This was a trap in which Una herself had felt caught. C.G. Jung wrote: 'It is not possible to live too long . . . in the bosom of the family, without endangering one's psychic health. Life calls us forth to independence.' This might have been written for and about Stella Manners or Una Marson, women whose wild natures called them out into the world" (*Life*, 132).

Marson's fourth volume of poems and final complete creative work, *Towards the Stars* (1945), had both new poems and poems culled from previous collections. Thematically, the new poems dealt with the bleakness of the war years and Marson's awareness of racism. In this collection, Marson is no longer preoccupied with the "desolate woman" persona. The lonely woman protagonist appears in only one poem. Instead, the reader is now exposed to Marson's resentment toward the white British. Her "increasing interaction with whites it seems, only increased her bitterness".[38] In "Politeness", Marson does not censor her obvious animosity toward white bigotry:

> They tell us
> That our skin is black
> But our hearts are white.
> We tell them
> That their skin is white
> But their hearts are black.
> (*Towards*, 44)

In a contradictory way, Marson derogatorily uses the colour "black" to describe the hatred that whites held for the black race and uses the colour "white" to suggest the purity of black people's hearts, despite the blackness of their skin. Arguably, Marson's education, which demonized blackness, subconsciously resided within her and is the same whitewashing that she cautions her persona from absorbing in her poems. This perhaps was unavoidable given her many years of colonial education.

Towards the Stars also revealed Marson's discontent with humanity and the tragic emotional impact the war had on her. During the war, she was less vocal about her feminist and racial concerns and, on occasion, she was poetically silent, as expressed in "Frozen Winter 1941"; "The heart of humanity is frozen / It is too cold for Poets to sing" (*Towards*, 45). Marson's anguish from the Second World War is heard further in "They Come no More", where she laments that "men must die / For liberty" (*Towards*, 52). Marson also displayed her spiritual side in this collection, which might have been her way of consoling herself during the war. "For There Will Come a Time" envisions racial equality:

> For there will come
> A time when all the races of the earth,
> Grown weary of the inner urge for gain,
> Grown sick of all the fatness of themselves
> And their boasted prejudice and pride,
> Will see this vision
> (*Towards*, 62–63)

Spending much of her time working in solitude, Marson affirms the pinnacle of self-realization in the title poem "Towards the Stars" about "the need to survive alone":

> Man must stand
> Alone
> Firmly planted
> in Humanity
> and grow
> Towards the stars.
> (*Towards*, 40)

By the 1950s and 1960s, however, we see Marson's ideas about matrimony transformed and, while she resided in the United States, she was briefly married. In fact, Marson, in her fifties, takes a radical turn in her liberal feminist views when she states that "marriage is a career or should be" (*Life*, 204). In the article "Have Married Women Taken the Wrong Turning", Marson, contrary to her lifelong commitment to feminist politics, argues against gender equality in marriage, child-rearing and sexual politics. She concludes that "'in the hot pursuit of happiness' woman probably had taken the wrong turning" (*Life*, 204). In this way, Marson, strangely, had come to see the home as the rightful place of women, once they had children under ten years old.

It is apparent that Marson's poetic canon followed a trajectory of her life experiences and transitions. Her writing is a testament to her political activism and, in some instances, to her personal life. She never separated her creative pursuits from her personal experiences. Her poetry and dramatic work symbolically ushered in a new era in Jamaica's literary landscape. Britain's hold on Jamaica's cultural imagination would finally be challenged by artists like Marson who were eager to free their nation of colonial authority and cultural dominance.

The late 1930s labour rebellions across the anglophone Caribbean marked the start of this nationalist movement. Jamaican artists, boldly steered by the likes of Marson, worked to foster an acceptance of African retentions on the island in order to counteract centuries of British cultural influence, especially among the elite. Marson knew that reversing the stigma against African religious practices, politicizing black self-love and embracing an African Jamaican aesthetic in her literary work would play a significant role in advancing the nationalist project. In championing a national literature, Marson used her characters, settings and themes to evoke the full spectrum of Jamaican society and those she met through her travels. Marson also gave us a glimpse into her life to understand the collective struggles of her people. But, as Honor Ford-Smith succinctly puts it, "What emerges from the best of Marson's creative work is that she attempted to voice the contradictions which she experienced in her own life. Most importantly, she used her personal experience as the raw material for her work."[39]

Indeed, Marson's life experiences served as raw material for her creative work since her writing "as a whole represents a movement from one era to the next".[40] Her earlier writing spoke to her insecurities and the colonial education that affected her craft and tainted how she saw herself as a black Jamaican woman. Marson's later creative work, however, represented a new poetic style that responded paradoxically to her inclusion and isolation in British society. Her later work also demonstrated how she challenged the social expectations of what women should and could write. Ultimately, Una Marson's writing provided her with a new perspective on herself as she found pride in her heritage as an African Caribbean person.

NOTES

1. Brown, *West Indian Poetry*, 7.
2. Tomlinson, "Una Marson: An Anticolonial Feminist".
3. Jarrett-Macauley, *Life of Una Marson*, 1. Hereafter cited parenthetically in the text as *Life*.
4. "Are Our Secondary Schools Snob Centres?", n.d. (Una Marson Papers, Box 1944B, National Library of Jamaica).
5. Marson, *Tropic Reveries*, 70. This and all books by Marson are hereafter cited in the text using short titles.
6. Marson, "Are Our Secondary Schools Snob Centres".
7. Rosenberg, "Modern Romances", 170.
8. Smilowitz, "Una Marson", 62–68.
9. Ford-Smith, "Una Marson", 26.
10. Smilowitz, "Marson, Rhys, and Mansfield", 104.
11. Cited in King, *West Indian Literature*, 2–3.
12. Swanzy, "Literary Situation", 249.
13. Naipaul, *Middle Passage*, 13.
14. Moore, *Chosen Tongue*, 40.
15. Donnell, "Una Marson", 123.
16. Una Marson, "Problems of Coloured People in Britain", n.d. (Una Marson Papers, Box 1944C, National Library of Jamaica, Kingston), 1.
17. Hill, *Jamaican Stage*, 272–73.
18. Donnell, "Una Marson", 131.

19. Ibid., 122.
20. Oakley, "Ideas", 92.
21. Tomlinson, "Una Marson: Cultural and Literary Nationalist".
22. See Thompson, "Black Skin", 11.
23. Letter to Mr Fletcher, n.d. (Una Marson Papers, Box 1944, National Library of Jamaica).
24. "Wartime in Britain", n.d. (Una Marson Papers, Box 1944, National Library of Jamaica).
25. Baxter, *Arts of the Island*, 84–85.
26. Snaith, "Little Brown Girl", 108.
27. Procter, "Una Marson", 2.
28. Hendy, "Caribbean Voices".
29. "The America I Have Discovered", n.d. (Una Marson Papers, Box 1944A, National Library of Jamaica).
30. King, *Reggae*, 70.
31. Smilowitz, "Marson", 137.
32. Cobham, "Women", 205.
33. Brown, *West Indian Poetry*, 34.
34. Tomlinson, *African-Jamaican Aesthetic*, 57.
35. Smilowitz, "Marson, Rhys, and Mansfield", 131.
36. Ibid., 122.
37. Campbell, "Unpublished Plays", 30.
38. Smilowitz, "Marson, Rhys, and Mansfield", 130.
39. Ford-Smith. "Una Marson", 28.
40. Brown, *West Indian Poetry*, 37.

BIBLIOGRAPHY

Baxter, Ivy. *The Arts of an Island. Metuchen, NJ: Scarecrow, 1970.*

Brown, Lloyd W. *West Indian Poetry.* Boston: Twayne, 1976.

Campbell, Elaine. "The Unpublished Plays of Una Marson". In *Anglophone Karibik–USA: Peripherie und Zentrum in der "neuen welt"*, edited by Michael Hoenisch and Remco van Capelleveen, 110–16. Hamburg: Argument-Verlag, 1991.

Cobham, Rhonda. "Women in Jamaican Literature 1900–1950". In *Out of the Kumbla: Caribbean Women and Literature, edited* by Carole Boyce Davies and Elaine Savory Fido, 195–222. Trenton, NJ: Africa World Press, 1990.

Donnell, Alison. "Una Marson: Feminism, Anti-colonialism and a Forgotten Fight for Freedom". In *West Indian Intellectuals in Britain*, edited by Bill Schwarz, 114–31. Manchester: Manchester University Press, 2003.

Fanon, Frantz. *Black Skin, White Masks.* Translated by Charles Lam Markmann. New York: Grove, 2004.

Ford-Smith, Honor. "Una Marson: Black Nationalist and Feminist Writer", *Caribbean Quarterly.* 34, nos 3–4 (1988): 22–37.

Hendy, David. "Caribbean Voices". https://www.bbc.co.uk/historyof thebbc/people-nation-empire/caribbean-voices. Accessed 15 April 2019.

Hill, Errol. *The Jamaican Stage, 1655–1900: Profile of a Colonial Theatre.* Amherst: University of Massachusetts Press, 1992.

Jarrett-Macauley, Delia. *The Life of Una Marson, 1905–65*. Manchester: Manchester University Press, 1998.

King, Bruce. *West Indian Literature*. London: Macmillan, 1995.

King, Stephen A. *Reggae, Rastafari, and the Rhetoric of Social Control*. With contributions by Barry T. Bays III and P. Renée Foster. Jackson: University Press of Mississippi, 2002.

Marson, Una. *Heights and Depths: Poems*. Kingston: Gleaner Company, 1931.

———. *The Moth and the Star*. Kingston: The author, 1937.

———. *Pocomania and London Calling*. Kingston: Blouse and Skirt Books, 2017.

———. *Towards the Stars*. Bickley, Kent: University of London, 1945.

———. *Tropic Reveries*. Kingston: Gleaner Company, 1931.

Moore, Gerald. *The Chosen Tongue: English Writing in the Tropical World*. London: Longmans, 1969.

Naipaul, V.S. *The Middle Passage*. New York: Vintage, 1981.

Oakley, Leo. "Ideas of Patriotism and National Dignity" [1970]. In *The Routledge Reader in Caribbean Literature*, edited by Alison Donnell and Sarah Lawson Welsh, 91–93. London: Routledge, 1996.

Procter, James. "Una Marson at the BBC". *Small Axe*, no. 48 (November 2015): 1–28. https://doi.org/10.1215/07990537-3341693.

Rosenberg, Leah. "Modern Romances: The Short Stories in Una Marson's 'The Cosmopolitan' (1928–1931)". *Journal of West Indian Literature* 12, nos. 1–2 (2004): 170–83.

Smilowitz, Erika. "Marson, Rhys, and Mansfield". PhD dissertation, University of New Mexico, 1984.

———. "Una Marson: Woman before Her Time". *Jamaica Journal* 16, no. 2 (1983): 62–68.

Snaith, Anna. "Little Brown Girl in White, White City: Una Marson and London". *Tulsa Studies in Women's Literature* 27, no. 1 (2008): 93–114.

Swanzy, Henry. "The Literary Situation in Contemporary Caribbean" [1956]. In *The Routledge Reader in Caribbean Literature*, edited by Alison Donnell and Sarah Lawson Welsh, 249–52. London: Routledge, 1996.

Thompson, Krista A. " 'Black Skin, Blue Eyes': Visualizing Blackness in Jamaican Art, 1922–1944". *Small Axe*, no. 16 (2004): 1–31. https://doi.org/10.1215/-8-2-1.

Tomlinson, Lisa. *The African-Jamaican Aesthetic: Cultural Retention and Transformation across Borders. Leiden: Brill/Rodopi, 2017.*

———. "Una Marson: An Anti-Colonial, Feminist, Anti-Racist, Pan-Africanist Champion of Good Causes". 19 March 2014. http://www.thefeministwire.com/2014/03/una-marson-anti-colonial-feminist-anti-racist-pan-africanist-champion-good-causes.

———. "Una Marson: Cultural and Literary Nationalist". *African American Intellectual History Society*. 26 March 2016. https://www.aaihs.org/una-marson.

ACKNOWLEDGEMENTS

As always, many thanks to my dearest mother, Gwendolyn Ewers-Tomlinson, for planting the seed and nurturing the love I have for my culture. Mom, your love and guidance are with me in whatever I pursue.

I also wish to thank my siblings, Corneal, Sherldine (Diane) and Karen Tomlinson, for allowing me to share the life and work of Una Marson with them. The endless conversations we had throughout the years have helped me to flesh out ideas and critical thoughts about Marson's work and life.

I am forever grateful to Carolyn Cooper for providing me with this golden opportunity to fulfil my dream of writing about my favourite literary and cultural icon, Una Maud Marson.

I would like to express my gratitude towards my colleagues and friends, Schontal Moore and Ajamu Nangwaya, for encouraging me to take on this writing project. Thanks, Ajamu, for the many times I disrupted your workflow in the office just to talk about Una Marson. Your feedback was helpful.

ACKNOWLEDGEMENTS

I would also like to express my gratitude to Andrew Allen, Donna Hope and Jennifer Robinson for checking in regularly on the progress of the book. Jennifer, thanks especially for listening to me read sections of the manuscripts at all hours of the night. Andrew, I am greatly appreciative of the multiple times you helped me to search for Una Marson's Old Hope Road residence, which we discovered months later was minutes away from where I live.

Shanik Wright, thanks for helping me to access the additional material for this project.

www.ingramcontent.com/pod-product-compliance
Lightning Source LLC
Chambersburg PA
CBHW032023090426
42741CB00006B/717